SYMPHONY™
Made Easy
ROBERT • WOLENIK

SYMPHONY™
Made Easy

ROBERT • WOLENIK

CBS Computer Books

HOLT, RINEHART AND WINSTON
*New York Chicago SanFrancisco Philadelphia
Montreal Toronto London Sydney Tokyo
Mexico City Rio de Janeiro Madrid*

First distributed to the trade in 1985 by Holt, Rinehart and Winston General Book Division

Library of Congress Cataloging in Publication data

Wolenik, Robert.
  Symphony made easy.

  Includes index.
    1. Symphony (Computer program)   2. Business—Data
processing. I. Title.
HF5548.4.S95W65   1985   001.64′25   85-5859
ISBN 0-03-002152-9

Printed in the United States of America

Published simultaneously in Canada

 67 039 9 8 7 6 5 4 3 2

CBS COLLEGE PUBLISHING
Holt, Rinehart and Winston
The Dryden Press
Saunders College Publishing

Trademark Acknowledgements

Table of Contents

Special Note to the Reader

This book is a tutorial guide to SYMPHONY, not a general specification of the software as delivered to the buyer now or in future software revisions. It was written and produced independently of Lotus Development Corporation, Inc. which has neither sponsored nor approved it. While all reasonable precautions have been taken to assure that this book is as accurate and current as possible at the time of writing, the author assumes no responsibility for omissions or errors. Software manufacturers occasionally update and change their products. Therefore, no guarantee of any kind is given regarding information and directions in the text and no liability is assumed by the author for any damages resulting from the use of information contained in this book.

Lotus Development Corporation, Inc. makes no warranties with respect to this book or to its accuracy in describing any version of the SYMPHONY software product.

Introduction

If you are new to Symphony, the most important thing to remember is, *Don't Be Intimidated*!

Symphony is a *big* program, but it is *not* a difficult program to learn or to use. With a proper introduction there's no reason you can't be doing word processing, spreadsheet modeling, data processing, or a combination of these or other applications, within the first hour of use.

I have found that a helpful way to think of the user of Symphony is as a conductor of an orchestra:

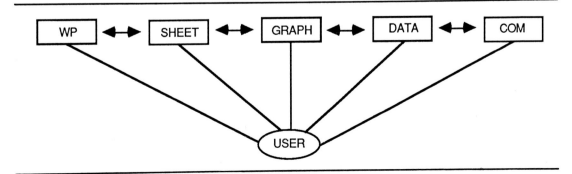

In this analogy the orchestra has five sections:

- Word Processing

- Spreadsheet

- Graphics

- Data Processing

- Communications

As conductor, you can choose which section you want to perform and which section you want to be silent. Or you can create a blend of different sections.

More importantly, you can choose whether to have your orchestra play loudly (at full capacity) or softly (just minimum capacity).

Without stretching this analogy too thin, I simply want to emphasize that as users of Symphony, we can operate the program at a very basic level, or we can delve deeper and play Symphony at a highly sophisticated level.

It is up to the user to choose how simple or how complex he or she wants Symphony to be. (We'll see how this works in later chapters.)

Learning the Command Structure

Symphony has hundreds of commands, more than you would ever want, or need, to memorize. These commands give the user the option of intricately controlling whatever application is being used. However, it is possible to use Symphony quite well with only 10 or 15 percent of these commands. What's more, Symphony is a "smart" program. In certain critical areas it actually comes to your aid. For example, if you want to make a graph, Symphony will step in and help do the dirty work. All you need to do is tell it where the data is, and it will virtually create the graph for you. Similarly, if you need a form for data processing, Symphony will create one for you. You just tell it the nature of the information you're going to enter. As you explore Symphony, you'll discover even more areas where the program almost seems to "think" for you.

Starting an Adventure

In fact, the proper attitude for learning Symphony is to think of yourself as participating in a grand and exciting adventure. You may make a few false turns, but each step will bring you closer to the tasks you want to accomplish with Symphony.

Using This Book

This book is organized to get you up and running on Symphony in the fastest way possible. The next chapter gives you an overview of the arrangement of *menus* within Symphony, which you will need to know before starting.

After that, you should turn to any particular section you want. Each section has an explanation of the task to be accomplished, as well as instructions on how to accomplish it.

This Book as a Reference

In addition to teaching you Symphony, this book is also designed to be used as a handy reference after you've learned the program. Explanations are given in simple **Task/Command/Explanation** format that allows you to quickly determine the answer to a specific question.

Overcoming Intimidation

Remember, the most important thing is to feel comfortable with Symphony. Anxiety can get in your way more than anything else. Don't fret with such worries as, "I don't know where to start!" or, "It doesn't make sense!"

This book will show you where and how to start, and you'll see very quickly what remarkable sense Symphony makes.

CHAPTER
1

Up and
Running!

The most practical way to learn a program is to start with the menus (for those new to programs, menus are simply lists of commands you can give to make the program perform certain operations.) It helps to think of the menu structure as a pyramid. The Main Menu is at the top. Below it are more specific menus, and below these even more specific ones. *Get the menu structure worked out and you'll quickly understand the program,* is an old user's adage.

Well, yes and no.

Symphony has menus with a structure similar to that just described. However, simply learning the menus Symphony uses isn't that helpful when you want to get up and running.

Rather, Symphony is like an onion. You first learn the surface. Then you can peel it away to reveal a new and more complex layer, which can in turn be peeled away revealing yet another layer, and so on.

I'm emphasizing this because, as you go through this book, you'll find that it's not organized according to Symphony's menus. Instead, it's organized according to the task you want to perform. I believe that as you peel away the onion skins you'll see the advantages of doing things this way.

First Things First

Presumably you've purchased your copy of Symphony and are ready to get started. To begin, you must make *back-up copies* of all the Symphony diskettes. The instructions that come with the program are straightforward and can be easily followed.

Next you need to "install" your program. This is a bit trickier. The instructions that come with Symphony lead you right up to the INSTALL program and then disappear. They assume that you can get everything you need to know from the screen.

Again, yes and no. I suggest that you work your way through the INSTALL program, making each choice according to your best guess. Then try running Symphony. If it works the way you want, great. If not, you can always go back and try installing it a second time.

Install Hints

The following are some points to keep in mind as you install Symphony. First you must have the right hardware to run Symphony. Just having an IBM or COMPAQ brand computer may not be enough. Your computer must have:

1. A *minimum* of 320K in RAM ("Random Access Memory"). The more RAM, the better the program will function, as we'll see later. 512K in RAM is a good choice.

2. A graphics card (if you want to see graphics).

3. A graphics capable screen (again, if you want to see graphics).

4. A color card and a color screen (if you want to see Symphony in color).

5. A graphics capable printer (if you want to be able to print graphics).

You are given 14 choices for your video driver in the INSTALL program. Figure 1.1 displays the program's INSTALL MENU.

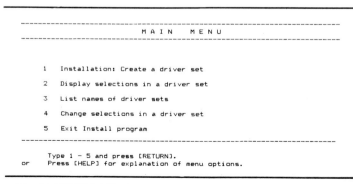

```
------------------------------------------------------------------------
                          M A I N    M E N U
------------------------------------------------------------------------


        1    Installation: Create a driver set

        2    Display selections in a driver set

        3    List names of driver sets

        4    Change selections in a driver set

        5    Exit Install program
    ----------------------------------------------------------------

         Type 1 - 5 and press [RETURN].
    or   Press [HELP] for explanation of menu options.
```

Fig. 1.1 INSTALL MENU

When working with the INSTALL program you need to keep the following hints in mind:

1. If you can't find your hardware listed, take a guess on something that sounds close. Chances are it will work. If it doesn't, you can come back and try INSTALL a second (or even a third time).

2. The difference between *toggle* and *shared* mode is important. With toggle mode, you'll be able to see *either* graphics or text, but not both at the same time. With shared mode *both* graphics and text will appear on your screen. (Of course, you still need the proper hardware to see any graphics.) The toggle mode gives you the greatest clarity for text.

In the INSTALL program, *you can make more than 1 selection* when you are asked to name your graphics printer. For example, you could choose the Epson FX printer in Density 1, Density 3 and Density 4. (Making additional selections, however, uses up additional disk space.)

When you are asked for your text printer in the INSTALL program, be careful of your selection. There are dozens of printers listed, including several generic varieties. The generic choice might be your best bet. For example, I chose the selection for the Epson, RX and FX printers. I found that this selection drove the RX printer quite well, but would not adequately operate the FX printer. The generic parallel printer driver, however, worked all printers adequately.

Firing It Up!

Now that you've successfully installed Symphony, it's time to fire it up.

Assuming you've got a double disk drive, turn on your computer and put Symphony in the A drive. If you are using a hard disk, then get to Symphony.

To call up the program, just type:

SYMPHONY

It will boot up, provided that you have installed a LOTUS driver. If you have installed another driver you'll need to type:

SYMPHONY (plus the driver's name)

For example, I have a second driver I call "Color" on which I've installed color. When I write SYMPHONY, the default Lotus driver I've installed calls up the program in black and white. When I type SYMPHONY COLOR, the second driver is accessed and the program comes up in color.

Symphony also has a pilot program called ACCESS, which you can call up. It then directs you to Symphony. I find this an unnecessary extra step, however.

Your First View

After the credits and introductory material, your first view of Symphony should look like (you should now have Symphony on your screen to proceed further with this book):

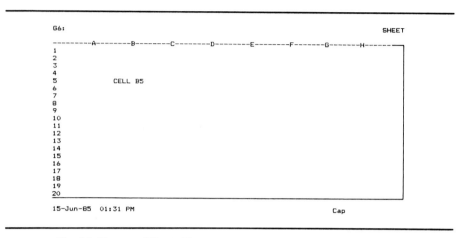

Fig. 1.2 Diagram of Empty Sheet.

If you've never used a spreadsheet, or if you're new to Symphony, it can be pretty disconcerting. You may want to know where all the menus are. Or you may want to know how to find word processing or data processing.

Symphony could start with a basic menu that reads:

1. SPREADSHEET

2. WORD PROCESSING

3. GRAPHICS

4. DATA PROCESSING

5. COMMUNICATIONS

This would then alert you to your options. However, it doesn't. (Once you get going in Symphony, such a menu constantly popping up every time you switched environments, would be a nuisance and a time waster.)

This type of menu does exist however. Let's go to it now. Hit [**ALT**] *then* [**F10**]. (All keys are based on the IBM keyboard.) The upper left hand corner of your screen should now display the five applications available with Symphony:

Spreadsheet work environment
SHEET DOC GRAPH FORM COMM

The top line tells you that you are now in a spreadsheet environment. The second line tells you that you can select any of the other environments listed.

Making a Selection from a Menu

You make a selection in one of two ways. Either use the arrow keys to move the pointer to your choice and then hit [**ENTER**]. *OR* select the first letter of your choice. Either way, Symphony will take you where you want to go. *Note*: this is the procedure for making a selection from a menu throughout Symphony.

Try it now. Select DOC.

You'll see the screen switch slightly. (In the chapters on word processing you'll learn what the different borders mean and how to use them.) Now switch back to SHEET, *but* don't use the menu. This time use [**ALT**] *then* [**F9**]. (I say *then* instead of *plus* because I've found that hitting the second key just a fraction of a second after the first, works better than hitting them simultaneously.)

You've just used the "switch" keys. They will "toggle" you back and forth between *the last two environments* that you used. "Switch" again [**ALT**] + [**F9**]. Note that you're back in the DOC environment. This switching is very helpful, as we'll see later on.

Now try going to the other environments, GRAPH, FORM and COMM. (Remember, use [**ALT**] + [**F10**]).

If you don't see anything, don't be alarmed. The windows come up blank because you haven't entered any data. In the separate sections on the different Symphony programs you will learn how to quickly use each one.

Getting Out of Menus

Let's try something different. This time "switch," but do not make a selection. Let's assume you accidentally hit the keys. How do you return to where you were?

Symphony uses the [**ESC**]ape key to go back to a previous window. *In any menu you can get back to the previous window by hitting* [**ESC**]. (In some menus, in fact, it's the only way out. Many menus do, however, provide a "Quit" option to take you back to where you were.)

If you try to execute an "illegal" command (one that isn't on the menu) of a window you are in, Symphony will indicate **ERROR** and "beep". Usually the solution is to hit [**ESC**]. It will take you out of the menu and back to where you started.

The Enter Key

While we are on the subject of keys, let's cover one other that has a special meaning, *the carriage return*. This is the one with the angled left arrow on the IBM keyboard.

Besides being used as a carriage return for word processing, this key is also used to *enter information*. Therefore, it is frequently referred to as the [**ENTER**] key.

The Services Menu

Now that you've had a brief tour of Symphony's different environments, let's take a look at some of the services that Symphony offers in each of them. Get to the SERVICES MENU by hitting [**F9**]. You should see:

WINDOW FILE PRINT CONFIGURATION APPLICATIONS SETTINGS NEW EXIT

If Symphony had a MAIN MENU (after the WINDOW MENU we've already looked at) this would be it. This menu lists many of the routine operations you'll want to perform. Let's look at just a few of them:

WINDOW — Controls Symphony's windowing, explained in Chapter 8.

FILE — Controls Symphony's file management system (which saves what you've created). It is discussed in Chapter 17.

PRINT — Controls printing, which is discussed in various chapters, notably 10 and 17.

CONFIGURATION, APPLICATIONS, SETTINGS — Discussed with file management in Chapter 17.

NEW — A powerful command. Use it to erase whatever you have in current memory and start with a clean slate. (Be sure to first "save" important data.)

EXIT — Takes you out of the SERVICES MENU. *Note*: you can operate Symphony satisfactorily knowing only a fraction of the commands on this menu, which is why the menu isn't fully explained here. What is important to understand is that SERVICES is the generic menu that operates in each Symphony environment whether it is DOC, SPREADSHEET, GRAPH, FORM or COMM.

Environment Menu

In addition to the SERVICES MENU, I want to mention one other menu in this chapter—the ENVIRONMENT MENU. This is accessed by hitting [**F10**].

Called simply "MENU" for short, it lists commands specific to an *environment*. For example, go to the DOC environment. (Remember how? Use the "switch" keys [**ALT**] + [**F10**].) Now hit the [**MENU**] key ([**F10**]). Immediately at the top of the screen will appear a menu of commands you can use for word processing (Figure 1.3).

```
Copy block of text                                                    MENU
Copy   Move   Erase   Search   Replace   Justify   Format   Page   Line-Marker   Quit
```

Fig. 1.3 Document Menu Commands.

Now switch to the GRAPH environment. Once there, hit the [**F10**].

Notice that the menu now displayed is different (Figure 1.4). This is the menu for graphs (explained in detail in the chapters on graphing).

```
Display a graph in this window                          MENU
Attach   1st-Settings   2nd-Settings   Image-Save
```

Fig. 1.4 Graph Menu Commands.

In other words, whenever you hit [**F10**], what is displayed will depend on which environment you are in. Symphony has five different sets of menus, one for each of its environments.

Services vs. Menu

Let's review. The SERVICES MENU ([**F9**]) is the same for every environment. But the (Environment) MENU ([**F10**]) is different for each environment.

Diskette Placement

If you are running a two-diskette system, you should note that once Symphony is loaded from your Symphony diskette, you may remove the Symphony diskette and store it. The program normally does not need to access the diskette again.

In the drive from which you removed it, (presumably the "A" drive), you can place either the HELP/TUTORIAL diskette (which will allow you to call up help as needed) or a blank data diskette on which you will save whatever you create in Symphony.

First-time users might find that having HELP/TUTORIAL in A, with data in B is the most useful arrangement. However, after awhile you'll want to keep your data diskette in A to make it easier to save and retrieve material.

How This Book Works

Throughout this book the following format is used to explain Symphony functions:

Task — Describes the job to be accomplished.
Command — Gives the commands needed to get the job done.
Explanation — Explains both what the job involves and how the command works.

This is straightforward and should present no problems. However, a word should be said about how a *command* is expressed.

Symphony is a menu-oriented program. To get to a particular command, you may have to go through several menus. For example, here's a typical command to set the left margin in a document:

Command – DOCUMENT, MENU, FORMAT, SETTINGS, LEFT

Translated, this means that in order to set the left margin, the following must be done in this precise order (reading left to right):

1. Get to the DOCUMENT window.

2. Call up the MENU ([**F10**]).

3. Select FORMAT from the MENU.

4. Select SETTINGS from the FORMAT MENU.

5. Select LEFT from the SETTINGS MENU.

Displayed graphically it looks like this:

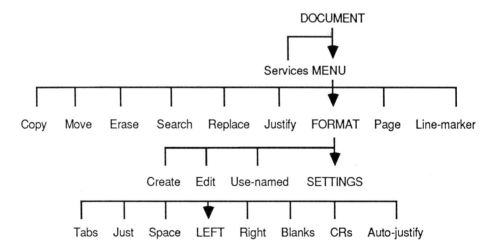

What we are doing is progressing through a series of menus until we reach the menu which contains the specific command we want. If this seems like threading our way through a maze, it is. However, after using Symphony for a while, the logic of the maze will break through, and you'll find it no problem at all to locate the exact command you want.

At the beginning, however, just follow the commands in the order indicated, from left to right, on the **Command** lines shown in this book.

≡Summary

And there you have it! You've just received an overview of the basic menu structure of Symphony. In case it went by too quickly, the chart in Figure 1.5 will help you remember.

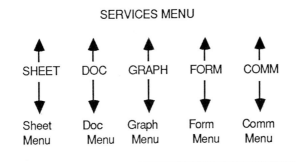

Each environment can get to either the common services menu or the individual environment menu.

SERVICES MENU

SHEET	DOC	GRAPH	FORM	COMM
Sheet Menu	Doc Menu	Graph Menu	Form Menu	Comm Menu

Fig. 1.5 Chart of environment, services menu, environment menu.

What we've done is to peel away the first layer of skin on our onion, to see the first surface of Symphony. You should now have enough information to be up and running. The next step is to select the environment you would like to start working in. It's usually best to start with word processing, which is very straightforward. However, if you have a spreadsheet or data processing task to perform, then don't hesitate to begin there. But you should NOT use the COMM (communications) environment until you have at least mastered the SPREADSHEET (because they are so interdependent).

When you have accessed the environment you want to work in, turn to the appropriate chapters in this book to find out how to get started.

Getting Started in Word Processing

Getting started in word processing is easy because it involves simple typing. If you already have some material on your screen, call up the SERVICES MENU and *save* what you have (we will look at saving at the end of this chapter). Now hit NEW.

To get to a document environment, hit **[ALT]** + **[F10]** and select DOC. You should see a clean document window. Now you're ready to begin writing. It doesn't matter if it's correspondence, a manuscript or a report. Just get a few lines on the screen. Figure 2.1 shows what your typing should look like.

As you go along, take note of a few things which are basic to word processing. First, when you reach the end of a line, *you do not need to hit a carriage return*. Symphony automatically wraps you around to the next line. If you've worked with word processors before, you'll recognize this as *wordwrap*. With wordwrap, in fact, it's important that you *don't* hit a carriage return unless you are at the end of a paragraph. (We'll see why this is when we look at reformatting.)

Notice also, the light square that moves along and indicates where you are typing. This is the cursor, which indicates the point at which the material you type is inserted

```
Change display characteristics of one or more windows            MENU
Use  Create  Delete  Layout  Hide  Isolate  Expose  Pane  Settings  Quit
     The document window is easily accessed by hitting the ALT + the F10
key on the IBM keyboard.  This calls up a selection of five
environments.  Simply select the desired one.
```

```
Window                                            Calc
```

Fig. 2.1 Illustration of a few lines in a DOC window.

onto the screen. The placement of the cursor is vital. It indicates where you will enter new words, and, as you'll see, it also allows you to delete errors. Let's take a closer look at what happens when the cursor is moved around.

Cursor Movement

The cursor can be moved in several ways. You can move it to your right one character place for each character or space typed. You can also use the arrow keys to move the cursor. It jumps one space for each single time the key is hit. Or you can hold the arrow keys down for repeated movements. Try it out on your screen.

Task — Move the cursor one word at a time
Command — CONTROL KEY PLUS LEFT OR RIGHT ARROW KEY
Explanation — Hold the [**CTRL**] (control) key down at the same time that you hit the *right or left* arrow key. The cursor will move along one word at a time. Lotus calls this "Big Left" and "Big Right."

Task — Move the cursor to the end or the start of a line
Command — END KEY PLUS LEFT OR RIGHT ARROW
Explanation — This will immediately take you to the end of the text on your line. *Note*: if there is a blank spot *before* the text begins, the cursor will move just to the beginning of the text. It will take another command to move it to the margin.

Task — Move cursor to the beginning or end of a paragraph
Command — END KEY PLUS UP OR DOWN ARROW
Explanation — the use of **[END]** + **[UP ARROW]** or **[END]** + **[DOWN ARROW]** will immediately take you to the beginning or end of your paragraph.

Task — Move cursor to the beginning or end of a document
Command — HOME KEY
Command — END KEY, HOME KEY
Explanation — to quickly get to the beginning of a document simply hit **[HOME]**. To get to the end of a document hit **[END]** + **[HOME]**. Figure 2.2 shows this cursor movement.

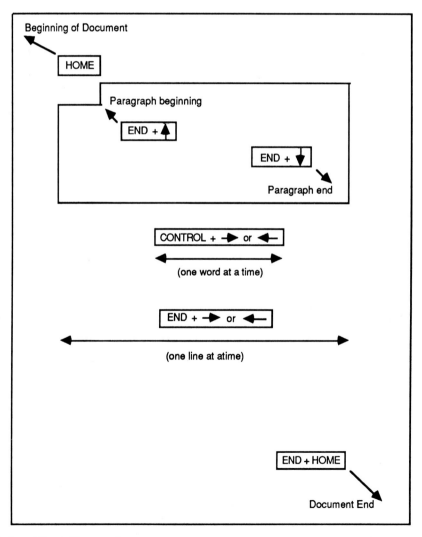

Fig. 2.2 Illustration of Cursor Movement.

There are several specific reasons for knowing how to move your cursor around. The most important is that the cursor lets you correct mistakes.

You can erase (delete) what you've written in a wide variety of ways. Here we'll consider only the simplest.

Task — Delete letters to left of cursor
Command — BACKSPACE KEY
Explanation — Place the cursor directly to the right of the letter(s) to be deleted. Then hit **[BACKSPACE]**. The cursor will move over the letter(s), erasing it. Hold the cursor down for repeated erasure.

This command can also be used to delete white space in front of a line in order to close up text.

Task — Delete letters to the right of the cursor
Command — DELETE KEY
Explanation — Place the cursor directly to the left of the letter(s) to be deleted. Then hit **[DELETE]**. The letter(s) will be drawn toward the cursor where it will be erased.

This command can also be used to delete white space behind text in order to close up open areas.

In addition to removing unwanted text by erasing, moving the cursor to a specific spot also allows you to enter new text exactly where you want it to go within a document.

Task — Insert new text into existing text
Command — MOVE CURSOR TO SPOT AND WRITE
Explanation — Make sure the INSERT key **[INS]** is *off*. (If it's *on*, an inverse OVR (overwrite) will be shown on the bottom of your screen.) Then, simply move new text to where you want it and type it in. It will force the old text back as it is entered. Then hit **[F2]** to reformat your paragraph.

Task — Insert new text while erasing old
Command — INSERT KEY
Explanation — This utilizes the *overwrite* feature, engaged through the **[INS]** key. To use it, hit **[INS]** so that OVR is displayed in inverse video on the lower right of your screen. Move your cursor to where you want to enter new material and erase old text. Then type. The new text will replace the old.

Task — Reformat a paragraph
Command — JUSTIFY (**[F2]**)
Command — DOCUMENT, MENU, JUSTIFY
Explanation — Symphony confuses the word *justification* with *reformatting*. (Justification refers to how text lines up with a margin. Reformatting refers to realigning text into a reasonable appearance after it has been edited.)

The best way to understand reformatting is to consider the following two paragraphs:

Jim and

Henry are partners

who worked hard   and

saved all their money.

This paragraph looks strange because it has been heavily edited, leaving words strewn all about the screen. Here is the same paragraph after it has been reformatted:

Jim and Henry were partners who
worked hard and saved all their money.

If you needed to do this reformatting yourself, it could be quite a chore. Symphony does it automatically, after you give certain commands (such as BLOCK COPYING, ERASE or MOVE). However, at other times, for example after using [**BACKSPACE**] or [**DELETE**], you may need to do the reformatting manually.

The easiest way to accomplish this is simply to be sure that the cursor is *anywhere* in the paragraph to be reformatted, then hit [**F2**]. Symphony will do the rest. *Note*: Symphony will only reformat between carriage returns. That's why it is important to make sure you don't have carriage returns at the end of sentences *within* a paragraph.

As an alternative, you can use the JUSTIFY command from the DOCUMENT MENU. Here you are asked if you want to reformat (justify) the current paragraph, or all the remaining paragraphs in the document. The latter command is very useful if you have made changes in several paragraphs and now want them all straightened out.

Working with Text

Thus far we've been discussing moving the cursor around the document. Now we're going to discuss moving the document itself around on the screen.

It's important when first learning the word processing program, to understand the difference between cursor movement and text movement. Although the distinction is simple, first-time users occasionally miss it.

Text Movement

Try typing a screenful of lines (20). This will take you to the bottom of the DOC window (presuming you haven't changed its size—see Chapter 8 on windowing.)

When your cursor reaches the end of the bottom line of text, the text will roll up, creating a new empty line in which to type. In this fashion, if you keep typing on the last line of your document window, the text will continue rolling up, one line at a time, as you require more room. This is the simplest way to move text on your screen. There are, however, several other ways of moving text.

Task — Move text up or down one full screen
Command — PAGE UP OR PAGE DOWN
Explanation — These commands will move the text up or down one full screen (up to 20 lines). You can hold these keys down and quickly browse through even a lengthy document.

However, one drawback is that this command automatically moves the cursor to the middle of the screen. That means that if you use [**PAGE UP**] to see what you have previously written, and then use [**PAGE DOWN**] to get back to where you are writing, you will probably find the cursor is in the wrong place. You'll have to move it back to where you want to insert text.

Task — Scroll up or down one line at a time
Command — SCROLL KEY PLUS UP OR DOWN ARROW
Explanation — The [**SCROLL LOCK**] key is a toggle. When it is *on*, the word SCROLL appears in inverse video on the lower right of your screen, and [**UP ARROW**] and [**DOWN ARROW**] keys no longer move the cursor. Instead they move the text up or down one line at a time. Hold the arrow keys down for repeated movement.

Task — Jump to text at right of screen
Command — SCROLL PLUS RIGHT OR LEFT ARROW
Explanation — The [**RIGHT ARROW**] key allows you to see text that is off to the right of the screen. The [**LEFT ARROW**] key brings you back. In Figure 2.3 you can see this movement.

Task — Go to a specific line of text
Command — GOTO ([**F5**])
Explanation — As you write a document, the line on which you are writing appears in the upper left hand corner of the screen. You can quickly go to any line of text by hitting the GOTO key [**F5**], and then entering the number of the line.

This command can also be used to go to a line-marker that you can leave embedded in the text. To embed a line-marker use the MENU, LINE-MARKER command and then follow the on-screen instructions.

Task — Find out where you are in relation to the printed page
Command — WHERE ([**ALT**] + [**F2**])
Explanation — Unfortunately, Symphony does not continuously display your printed page location in the text. To find out where you are you must use the WHERE command. It will then indicate on the lower left hand side of the screen, the page number and the line the cursor is on.

Scrolling to the right

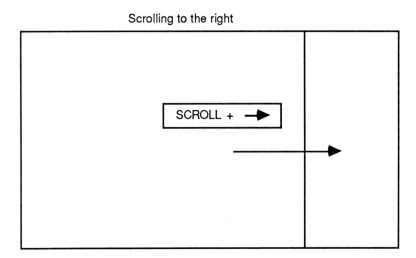

Fig. 2.3 Illustration of Scrolling.

Some Simple Editing Chores

Thus far we've seen how to handle the cursor and text, as well as how to delete and backspace over unwanted material. Now we're going to expand our horizons a bit and try some basic editing tasks.

Editing is another word for rewriting. It means going back and changing what you have already written. Text can be changed in a variety of ways including:

- Erasing
- Moving
- Copying

You've already seen how you can use [**DELETE**] or [**BACKSPACE**] to remove letters or words. However, when you want to delete more than just a word or two, these keys become impractical. For example, to remove an entire paragraph, you must hold down [**DELETE**] and wait, while the cursor backtracks over the paragraph, deleting it. You could also delete a paragraph and then retype it elsewhere, or type it twice if you want it to appear twice.

It should be apparent that the commands we have learned thus far are impractical for erasing, moving or copying larger blocks of text. That is why Symphony provides more powerful commands to handle larger chunks of material.

Task — Highlight text to be erased, moved or copied
Command — ARROW KEYS
Explanation — We'll get to the specific commands for erasing, moving and copying in a moment, but first you need to understand how to *highlight*, since this is the way to tell Symphony what is to be erased, moved or copied.

When you want to erase, copy or move (see the next set of tasks) you are told to indicate the text you want to handle. You should use your pointer to do this. When you do, you will find that the cursor is *anchored* to the location it was on before you issued the command. Now, using the arrow keys, you can highlight up, down, right or left from that anchor spot. To see exactly how this works, call up MENU, ERASE and then move the arrow keys. (To get out without erasing, hit [**ESC**] several times.) Figure 2.4 illustrates highlighting.

```
Copy block of text                                                    MENU
Copy  Move  Erase  Search  Replace  Justify  Format  Page  Line-Marker  Quit
    The document window is easily accessed by hitting the ALT + the F10
key on the IBM keyboard.  This calls up a selection of five
environments.  Simply select the desired one.
```

Fig. 2.4 Illustration of Highlighting.

To move the anchor:

Task — Move highlight anchor
Command — ESCAPE KEY, TAB KEY
Explanation — If you don't like where the cursor is anchored after invoking ERASE, MOVE or COPY, just hit the [**ESC**] key. Now you're free to move the cursor wherever you want. You can re-anchor it by hitting [**TAB**].

Task — Highlight quickly to the end of a sentence
Command — PERIOD KEY ([.])
Explanation — You can quickly highlight to the end of a sentence by hitting the *period* [.] once your cursor is anchored. The highlighting will move forward to the next period. This action can be repeated by hitting the [.]again.

Task — Highlight quickly to a letter
Command — LETTER
Explanation — This is one of Symphony's most powerful highlighting commands. You can highlight from the anchor spot to the next occurence of *any* letter, simply by typing in that letter. In this fashion, you can highlight portions of a sentence. For example:

| |This is an example of letter highlighting.

In the above sentence, by hitting the letter "e" (after invoking one of the block editing commands), the highlighting would extend from the anchor position to the beginning of the word "example."

Task — Erase unwanted text
Command — DOCUMENT, MENU, ERASE
Command — ERASE ([F4])
Explanation — As soon as you call up ERASE (you can either hit [F4], or use ERASE from the DOCUMENT MENU) you are asked:

Erase what block? 12,23. .12,23.

Symphony is asking what is to be erased. The numbers following the question refer to the line and the character that the cursor is on. You indicate what you want erased by highlighting (described above). The numbers indicate the *range* of text to be removed. (12,23. .13,5 = line 12, character 23 to line 13, character 5) As soon as you have highlighted the text hit the carriage return. The highlighted text will be gone **forever**!
Warning: be sure you want to erase the material. Once it's gone, it's gone for good.

Task — Move text
Command — DOCUMENT, MENU, MOVE
Explanation — Moving large or small blocks of text from one part of a document to another is a vital part of editing. Symphony makes the task easy.
As soon as the command is issued, Symphony asks:

Move FROM what block? 7,23. .7,23

You now use the pointer to highlight the text to be moved. Then hit the carriage return. Symphony now asks:

Move FROM what block? Ok   Move TO where: 12,5

"Ok" means it has the block to be moved. Now where does it go? Use the pointer to indicate where you want the text to be moved. You can indicate *any* spot in your document. (It doesn't have to be at the beginning of a line or in a blank space.)
Symphony will make the move and reformat the paragraph. Unfortunately, instead of leaving the cursor at the spot it was just moved to, it returns it to the spot it was moved from.

Task — Copy text
Command — DOCUMENT, MENU, COPY
Explanation — You can cause text to be "repeated" as often as you like with this command. It operates exactly like MOVE described above, except that the text both appears in a new spot and remains in the old spot.

Task — Turn off automatic reformatting after block change
Command — DOCUMENT, MENU, FORMAT, SETTINGS, AUTO-JUSTIFY
Explanation — Symphony automatically reformats a paragraph after every move, erase or copy action. You can turn off this feature by executing the above command.

≣A Complex Editing Chore

Now we come to two very useful editing techniques that can save you enormous time — SEARCH and REPLACE.

SEARCH is used to automatically find any word or portion of a word throughout a document. REPLACE is used to not only find a word or word portion, but also to replace it with another. (See Figure 2.5)

```
Substitute one character string for another                              MENU
Copy  Move  Erase  Search  Replace  Justify  Format  Page  Line-Marker  Quit

Replace what? Fred     Replace with what? Harry
```

Fig. 2.5 Search and Replace Menu.

Task — Find a word in a document
Command — DOCUMENT, MENU, SEARCH
Explanation — As soon as you issue this command, you are asked:

Search for what?

Type in what you're looking for. (What you type will appear at the top of your screen, not in the document.) You can enter as many as 50 characters. However, Symphony is very sensitive to upper and lower case commands. To find *all* occurrences, then, be sure to type everything that you are looking for in lower case.

Once you've told Symphony what to find, hit the carriage return. You are now asked whether you want the SEARCH to go forward or backward through the document. Indicate your preference.

Symphony will search until it finds the first occurrence of the word(s) you indicated, then it highlights. You can either continue to search (forward or backward) or quit.

When SEARCH can not find any other occurrences of the word(s) you want, Symphony "beeps" and the phrase "String not found" appears. (As we'll see in subsequent chapters, a "string" is any group of characters.)

Task — Replace a word(s) in a document
Command — DOCUMENT, MENU, REPLACE

Explanation — Here Symphony not only *finds*, but also *replaces*. To use this, you must first hit [**HOME**] to return to the beginning of a document (Symphony will only replace by going forward.)

Then, when you are at the beginning of your document, issue the REPLACE command. Symphony will now ask:

"Replace what?"

Type in an appropriate response.
Now Symphony will ask:

"Replace it with what?"

This time type in the replacement. Symphony will now automatically begin searching. As soon as it finds the first occurrence of the word (or string) you want replaced, it will highlight it and ask:

ONCE   CONTINUE   SKIP   ALL-REMAINING   QUIT

These questions are self-explanatory. You simply make your choice.

Saving Your Document

Saving what you've written is a vital part of the word processing program, as those already familiar with computers know. When you write a document, Symphony stores what you've written in the *RAM*, or *temporary memory* of the computer. As soon as the power is turned off, however, whatever is in RAM is immediately erased. That's why you need to *save* documents on the permanent memory of a disk. (Because of the chance of power failures, you should also save every screenful or several screens as you write.)

This is easy with Symphony. To save a document, just call up SERVICES MENU and select FILE.

Symphony will now give ten options. These will be discussed in detail in Chapter 17 on file management. For now, you need only be concerned with the first one, SAVE.

When SAVE is selected it asks:

Save file name:A: \

This is telling you that Symphony is ready to save the file in the A drive, and that it wants you to give it a name. (This is no problem if you have removed the Symphony diskette from the A drive and replaced it with a data diskette). But, if the data diskette is in B drive, or you are using a hard disk drive, you will need to specify the correct drive. To do this, be sure to use the format "Drive: \ ".

Up to eight characters of any name that appeals to you can be typed in. Now hit [**RETURN**] and Symphony will save the document on the disk.

Task — Save document while writing
Command — SERVICES, FILE, SAVE
Explanation — As noted earlier, to avoid losses when the power goes out, you should save your document periodically, as you are working on it. To do this the first time, just follow the instructions in the paragraph above.

There is a shortcut, however, for *repeated saves*. After you've saved your document once, and assuming your disk is in the A drive, follow this procedure:

1. Hit SERVICES, FILE, SAVE. The name you've selected for your document should now appear in the upper left window. Just hit carriage return once.

2. Symphony will now say, "A file with that name already exists. Replace it? Yes/No."

3. The file that exists is the one you already created with your first save. If you answer Y for "yes", Symphony will automatically erase the first save and put the current one in its place. This way you can constantly update your saves as you write.

Task — Retrieve a file
Command — SERVICES, FILE, RETRIEVE
Explanation — Use the pointer to highlight the file to be retrieved. (If more files exist than can be shown on the menu line, hit [F10] to display them on the screen). Then hit carriage return.

CHAPTER
3

Formatting
and Printing
Documents

Formatting, in the broad sense, refers to the *appearance* of a document. In this chapter, we're going to learn how to manipulate a document's appearance and then print the document out.

Formatting

Formatting can be divided into two distinct areas. The first is *on-screen formatting*, where we change the appearance of what we see right on the screen. The second is *off-screen formatting*. Here we change the appearance of the document as it will be printed out, but we can't see those changes on the screen; we have to wait until we get the printed page to see them.

Symphony does both. As long as you understand the difference between the two, they shouldn't be confusing when we work with them. Let's start with on-screen formatting, the most common formatting. The first thing that needs to be done is to set the margins (Figure 3.1).

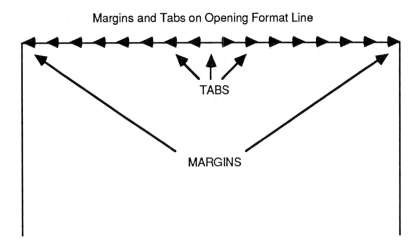

Fig. 3.1 Opening Format Line.

Margins

The margins, left, right, top and bottom, position the text in relation to the paper. Since Symphony is basically a "you get what you see" program, much of the formatting can be handled right on the screen.

At the top of the document window you will find a format ruler. The double arrows at left and right (<<   >>) indicate the current margins. The single right facing arrows indicate the current tab settings.

Task — Set left or right margin
Command — DOCUMENT, MENU, FORMAT, SETTINGS, LEFT/RIGHT
Explanation — This command sets the margins, as measured in characters from the left side of the screen. When you call up the left margin setting, you will find the default set at 1. You can change this to any other number (up to 240), as long as you don't go further right than the right margin.

When you call up the right margin you will find the default set at 72. You are given the choice of SET, to select a different number, or RESET, which sets the right margin back to the default of 72 characters.

Note: these settings determine the *width* of the document, but not necessarily its page location. The placement of the document on the page can be handled through the PRINT MENU, discussed in other chapters.

Tabs, Spacing and Justification

These are the other common formatting commands. Each comes set up with a default. The following commands change the default settings *within a document*. You can change the way the defaults come set up by reconfiguring Symphony (see Chapter 17).

Task — Clear or set tabs
Command — DOCUMENT, MENU, FORMAT, SETTINGS, TAB
Explanation — When you call up a document, you are shown a top ruler line that has tabs between the margins. It looks like this (Figure 3.2):

Margins and Tabs on Opening Format Line

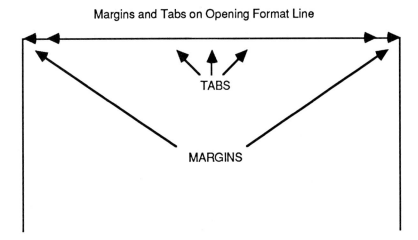

Fig. 3.2 Tabs cleared from format line.

To clear all tabs from the ruler line, call up the command and insert a tab setting larger than the line you are using (normally larger than 72). To change the tab intervals, specify the distance between tabs. To set tabs at uneven locations, use a new format line (discussed later in this chapter).

Task — Set spacing
Command — DOCUMENT, MENU, FORMAT, SETTINGS, SPACING
Explanation — This is simply how close the lines will be together *on the print-out*. The spacing on the screen is always single.

The default is set at single spacing. You can select up to triple spacing by choosing from the three numbers offered.

It is possible to get almost any spacing on Symphony, but it is tricky. You have to use single spacing, then give your printer a special line spacing command code, using the "init-string," when printing out. The init-string allows you to send a special command to the printer instructing it to double space (see later sections on printing). Then you must adjust the number of lines on the page for the size of the page you are using. (Check your printer's manual to see if it has this capacity.) If all this sounds overly complex just use the 1, 2, 3 spacing that Symphony offers.

Task — Set justification
Command — DOCUMENT, MENU, FORMAT, SETTINGS, JUSTIFICATION
Explanation — This command is different from that used to reformat a paragraph,

which is also called JUSTIFY. JUSTIFICATION asks whether the writing should line up flush with the left margin, should be even with both margins, or should be centered.

Here are four options:

NONE   LEFT   EVEN   CENTER

NONE turns off the justification. We will use this command when we edit forms created in our data processing environment. LEFT sets all type flush at the left margin. (This is the default setting). EVEN makes the type flush both left and right. CENTER puts the type down the center of the screen. Figure 3.3 gives examples of each.

```
Line 8     Char 53   Cell F8                          Left, Single              DOC

                     This is an example of text which has been
                     set flush left.  This is the standard
                     justification that Symphony uses
                     as a default.  Note the ragged right
                     margin and the justified left margin.




Line 2     Char 42   Cell E2                          Even, Single              DOC

                     This is an example of text which has been
                     set  "justified even"  on  both left  and
                     right  hand  sides.   This is  an  option
                     which  Symphony offers.   Note the  flush
                     left and right margins.




Line 10    Char 33   Cell D10                         Centered, Single          DOC

                         This is an example of text
                     which has been centered on the page.
                           Notice that the lines
                     are equal distant from both the left
                           and the right borders.
```

Fig. 3.3 Justification examples (3).

Visible and Invisible On-Screen Notes

With Symphony you can choose whether or not you want to view certain items on the screen. For example, you can choose whether or not to see actual blank spaces (represented by dots), or actual carriage returns (represented by left arrows).

Whether or not you want to see these items often depends on the kind of writing you're doing. If you are doing high-accuracy work, being able to count the specific number of blank spaces you have may be important. Knowing where a carriage return is located is also important in everyday writing because it helps in reformatting.

Task — Make blank spaces visible
Command — DOCUMENT, MENU, FORMAT, SETTINGS, BLANKS
Explanation — With this command you can elect to display the blanks as dots.

Task — Make carriage returns invisible
Command — DOCUMENT, MENU, FORMAT, SETTINGS, CR
Explanation — This command will make the carriage returns invisible, or will make them stand out as left arrows.

Using More Than One Format Within a Document

Thus far we have seen how to *set up* a document. However, we have been assuming that whatever format settings we have been using, we will want to continue to use throughout the text. That may not be the case, however.

For example, you may want some of your text to be double spaced, while other parts should be single spaced. Or, you may want some parts of the text to be flush left, other parts are to be centered.

Symphony provides a way to change the format anywhere in the document. This is done by inserting one or more new format lines. All text which *follows* the new format lines encompasses the new format. Perhaps an example will help:

```
L   T   T   T   T   T   T   T   T   T   RI1
```

This is the story of a small, brown dog who lived
in an abandoned shed by the side of the road.
His name was Rex, which stood for King, only he
didn't feel very "kingly" at all.

```
        L   T   T   T   RI2
```

Tommy Brown loved the

old dog Rex, but he

hadn't been able to find

him since they had moved

to the other side of

town and Rex had gotten

lost.

L   T   T   T   T   T   T   T   T   R I 1
Rex had spent a lot of days looking for Tommy
Brown, but the boy seemed to have vanished.
Strange new people were living in Tommy's house,
people who tried to catch him. Fortunately, he

Notice how the text in this story moves from single to double spacing and back, and also how the margins change. This is special formatting within a document.

You can accomplish this by creating new format lines (as shown). These new format lines will affect margins, spacing, justification and other items. It is important to understand, however, that they only affect the text that occurs *after them and until the next format line is specified.*

Task — Create a format line
Command — DOCUMENT, MENU, FORMAT, CREATE
Explanation — Symphony will ask where you want the format line to go. Place the cursor anywhere in the text. The format line will appear directly above the cursor line.

The new format line *will be a duplicate of the one just above it.* If this is the first format line you've created in your document, then it will duplicate the original document format line. If, however, this is a second, a third or another document line, then it will duplicate the *last* one you created. At some point, you will probably want to change the settings of this new format line. Notice that at the end of the format line there is a letter and a number (appearing after the R, which stands for "Right Margin"). The letter stands for the justification (L)eft, (E)ven, or (C)entered, and the number indicates the spacing (1, 2, or 3) on that format line.

Task — Change settings on the new format line
Command — (USE MENU ON SCREEN)
Explanation — As soon as you create a new format line you are shown the following menu:

MARGINS/TABS JUSTIFICATION SPACING LINE-MARKER USE-NAMED
    RESET QUIT

These settings apply *only* to the format line you are working on (and others linked to it, as we'll see later). The first three settings (MARGINS/TABS, JUSTIFICATION, SPACING) are the basic format commands, which we've already covered. We won't go over them in detail again, except to note a peculiarity when using MARGINS/TABS.

As soon as you hit the above command your screen will appear to go back to your document window, and it will seem as if you are writing text. Don't be fooled. Down at the bottom left of the screen will appear, "Format Create Margins/Tabs." You are still in the CREATE MENU. You need to use your arrow keys, [**BACKSPACE**] and [**DELETE**] to *move the margins and tabs you see on the screen* to where you want them. By actually moving the margins and tabs around, you create the format line you want.

Note: you can set the tabs *anywhere* on this new format line. This way you can have spacing which varies between tabs.

The RESET command is useful because it returns your format line to the original document settings. We will discuss the other settings under separate headings further on in the book.

Task — Reuse (name) a format line
Command — DOCUMENT, MENU, FORMAT, CREATE (OR EDIT), LINE-MARKER
Explanation — Sometimes you will want to use a format line with the same settings many times throughout a document (or other documents). Rather than continually creating new format lines, Symphony allows you to name an existing line and then simply call it up whenever you want to use its settings.

To do this you use the LINE-MARKER command from the format line, either with the GENERATE, or EDIT MENU. It asks what name you want to use. Simply write in any name (maximum of 15 characters).

Note: if you use an existing format line name, the old format line loses the name which the new line acquires.

Task — Copy a previously used named format line, and link it to the original
Command — DOCUMENT, MENU, FORMAT, CREATE, USE-NAMED
Explanation — After you create a new format, you may realize that you want it to have the exact same settings as some previously named (see the last task) format line. If this is the case, then simply hit the USE-NAMED command, which appears on the menu immediately after you have created a format.

This command will produce a directory of all format lines that you've named previously for this document. Simply point to the one you want and hit a carriage return.

When you indicate where the format line is to go, you will find that instead of a new format line appearing, the name of the first format line behind it will appear. For example, suppose you name your first format line, FIRST. Then you create a second format line, and want it to match the settings of FIRST. Select the USE-NAMED command and choose FIRST. On the left of the screen will appear:

FIRST

This tells you that you are using the settings in your format line named FIRST.

It's important to understand that both format lines you have now created are *linked*. If you edit the original format line, any changes you make to it *will automatically be made to all other format lines carrying its name.* If you edit the second format line you created, which carries the name of the original, then you break the link between the two. The secondary line loses the primary's name, and simply becomes a standard, unnamed format line.

Task — Create bordering format lines
Command — DOCUMENT, MENU, FORMAT, CREATE, HIGHLIGHT
Explanation — In the earlier example, in order to create text that was offset and spaced differently in the middle of a document, we needed two format lines, one at the beginning of the offset text, changing it from the document format, and one at the end, changing it back.

These are called "bordering formats," and can be created simultaneously. They are also easy to create. When you call up the command to generate a format line, instead of simply asking Symphony for a single format line by placing the cursor in one spot and then entering, place the cursor at the beginning or ending of your offset material and hit [**tab**] (which anchors it). Then *highlight* to the other end of the material. When you hit carriage return, two format lines will be created, bordering the offset material.

Task — Manipulating the format line
Command — DOCUMENT, MENU — MOVE, COPY, ERASE
Explanation — Like any other text, you can use the basic block movement commands to move a format line around your document.

Task — Kill the name of a format line
Command — DOCUMENT, MENU, LINE-MARKER, REMOVE
Explanation — If you don't want a particular format line to have a name, you can use this command to remove it. *Note*: removing the name does not remove the format line.

Indentation

The uses of format lines are almost too numerous to mention. As you become familiar with the procedures to create the lines, you will find yourself using them continually in your writing.

One feature that the format lines provide, but for which Symphony also has a shortcut, is *indentation*. Symphony has a special [**INDENT**] key ([**F3**]). It can be used to *temporarily* indent from the left margin. Figure 3.4 illustrates using the [**INDENT**] key.

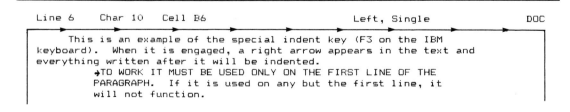

Fig. 3.4 Illustration of Indent.

Simply place your cursor where you want the left margin of a paragraph to be. Hit the indent key, ([**F3**]). It will put a right arrow on your screen. All text in a paragraph which follows (when reformatted) will be forced to the right of the arrow. But this applies *for one paragraph only.*

Special Print Features

Thus far we've been discussing formatting that can be seen on the screen. Now we'll turn to *off-screen formatting,* which is invisible on the screen, but which will appear when you print out. This refers to items such as boldface, italics, underlining and others.

Symphony cannot show you what these features will look like as you type. However, you can still incorporate them into the text by embedding codes which the printer can read. Assuming you have a printer which can handle these functions, the sheet you print out will then have boldface, italics, underlining and so forth. *Note*: not all printers can handle all these functions. You should select your printer from the list in the INSTALL MENU.

Task — Embed a print feature in text
Command — CONTROL B PLUS PRINT FEATURE
Command — CONTROL E
Explanation — This is the sort of thing that can make you pull your hair out and start screaming, until you get the hang of it. Then it becomes second nature. An example should help.

Suppose you want to set off a word with *boldface*. To accomplish this you would position the cursor at the beginning of the word. Then you would hit [**CONTROL**] [**B**].

This puts a small upside-down marker in the text. Now you can code in any one of 18 different codes. The code for Boldface is "**B**". Your total input is now, [**CONTROL**] [**B**] + [**B**]. Everything that is written after this code will now be in boldface.

To discontinue boldface you use a slightly different code. Place the cursor after the word(s) to be put in boldface and hit this sequence:

[**CONTROL**] [**E**]

This turns boldface off and returns you to regular type. The total picture looks like this (*Note*: be sure insert is "off", or else you'll overwrite text.):

CONTROL B + B = Bold type CONTROL E = End of boldface

Yes, it is a bit awkward, but it's far easier than what Lotus recommends, namely using the [**COMPOSE**] key, plus a double letter sequence. (*Turn on* equals [**ALT**] + [**F1**] + [**B**] + [**A**]!) Here are the most frequently used codes:

[**CONTROL**] [**B**] = turn on special print feature

[**CONTROL**] [**E**] = turn off special print feature

[**U**] = underline

[**B**] = Boldface

[**I**] = Italic

[**+**] = Superscript

[**−**] = Subscript

[**X**] = Strike through

Occasionally, you may want to combine some of these print features. Symphony provides a separate list of numbers for combining them:

```
9 = BOLD, ITALIC, SUPERSCRIPT
8 = BOLD, ITALIC, SUBSCRIPT
7 = ITALIC SUBSCRIPT
6 = BOLD SUBSCRIPT
5 = ITALIC SUPERSCRIPT
4 = BOLD SUPERSCRIPT
3 = ITALIC UNDERLINE
2 = BOLD ITALIC UNDERLINE
1 = BOLD UNDERLINE
0 = BOLD ITALIC
```

In addition, you can use S to apply the print functions to spaces, as well as characters. Q turns this function off.

Printing Out a Document

Printing a document is very easy with Symphony, *provided* your printer is hooked up correctly and ready to go. (Detailed instructions on printing are contained in Chapter 17. You should consult it now if you have problems or require special print commands.)

To print out a document, the first step is to call up the document. If you have some other document on the screen, *save it* and call up the one you want printed.

Once you've done this you are ready to begin printing. Your screen should look like Figure 3.5.

```
Change print settings                                                    MENU
Go  Line-Advance  Page-Advance  Align  Settings  Quit
```

Fig. 3.5 Print Menu.

Task — Start printer
Command — DOCUMENT, SERVICES, PRINT, GO
Explanation — When you call up the PRINT MENU you will be shown a settings sheet. To change any of the settings on the sheet, refer to Chapter 17.

If you are willing to accept the defaults Symphony provides, simply hit G for GO. Your printer will start working, and you'll have your document.

The margins (left and right) will be set according to your formatting inside the document (assuming you haven't set them beyond the limits of print default setting 76). The top and bottom margins will be set at two lines each. These may be changed from the PRINT, SETTINGS, MARGIN MENU.

The page length will be 66 lines, the starting page will be 1 and you will have a break at the end of each page. Unless you set them from the PRINT, SETTINGS, PAGE, HEADER/FOOTER commands, you will have no header, footer or page numbers. A sample of the print settings sheet is offered in Figure 3.6. (Again, if you want to make changes in any of the defaults, refer to Chapter 17 on printing.)

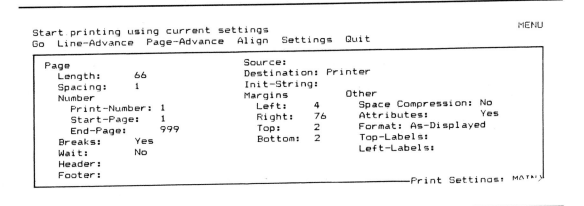

```
Start printing using current settings                          MENU
Go  Line-Advance  Page-Advance  Align  Settings  Quit

  Page                        Source:
    Length:      66           Destination: Printer
    Spacing:     1            Init-String:
  Number                      Margins           Other
    Print-Number: 1             Left:    4        Space Compression: No
    Start-Page:   1             Right:   76       Attributes:        Yes
    End-Page:     999           Top:     2        Format: As-Displayed
  Breaks:        Yes            Bottom:  2        Top-Labels:
  Wait:          No                               Left-Labels:
  Header:
  Footer:                                     Print Settings: MAIN
```

Fig. 3.6 Print Settings Sheet.

Task — Print out in a different pitch
Command — DOCUMENT, SERVICES, PRINT, SETTINGS, INIT-STRING
Explanation — Symphony offers no easy way to change the pitch of your print-out. (Typical pitches are *pica, elite, condensed* and *enlarged*.) If your printer has the capacity to print in pitches other than pica, however, you may set it up to do so by sending the appropriate printer control code. This is done through the INIT-STRING command.

You must first find out what the correct printer control code is, (look it up in your printer manual). Then, after calling up the INIT-STRING command, first enter a slash " \ " and then enter the code *in decimal form*. (Most printer manuals list it in symbol, decimal and hexadecimal.)

Once the INIT-STRING command has been given, Symphony will ask:

Printer control sequence:

Now just write in: Printer control sequence: \ 077
(Don't forget the slash " \ ")
Symphony will send the code to the printer, which will then print your document in elite pitch.

CHAPTER
4

Up and Running
in a Spreadsheet

The goal of this chapter is to give you enough information to quickly set up and use a spreadsheet. You'll learn how to get to a spreadsheet, how to move around it and how to handle entries; in other words how to manipulate it. In the next chapter we'll go into some more sophisticated uses for the spreadsheet.

What is a Spreadsheet?

The best definition of a spreadsheet that I've heard is that it is a "modeling device." However, if you don't already know what a spreadsheet is, this definition won't be too helpful.

It's easy to become confused because we are really asking two questions: "What does a spreadsheet do?" and "What does it look like?" First, let's figure out what it does.

What a Spreadsheet Does

If we're in business, the spreadsheet allows us to create a financial model. For example, it allows us to input our earnings by quarter so profits can be compared on a quarterly basis. It will also let us check inventory at three different warehouses so we can see which is most efficient. Or we can enter advertising expenses, as well as increases in revenue, so that we can see where our advertising dollars are most effective.

In other words, the spreadsheet allows us to "play with," or "model" the financial considerations of our business. (It's not limited to business, of course. Symphony's spreadsheet can also be adapted to scientific, mathematical, engineering and other modeling.)

What a Spreadsheet Looks Like

The best way to visualize the spreadsheet is as a piece of columnar paper, the sort that accountants use. It has numbered rows, as well as vertical columns. Figure 4.1 is an example of a typical *paper* spreadsheet.

The Electronic Spreadsheet

Symphony's spreadsheet is much like the paper one which appears at right, except that this *electronic* sheet is much larger. While a paper spreadsheet usually can display only a dozen columns, Symphony has 256 columns across the top, starting with A and going to IV. And, while a paper spreadsheet may have a maximum of 30 to 40 rows down the side of a page, Symphony has 8,192 rows.

The comparisons between an electronic and a paper spreadsheet become even more amazing. On both sheets, where a vertical column intersects a horizontal row, there is a spot to make an entry. This spot is called a *cell*. A paper spreadsheet with 20 columns and 30 rows has 600 cells.

Symphony, however, with 256 vertical columns and 8,192 rows, has an incredible total of 2,097,152 cells in the sheet. To get a better idea of this size, imagine that if Symphony's electronic spreadsheet could be laid out on paper, and each cell were one-half inch, by a half an inch tall, the paper would have to be over 10 feet wide, by over 340 feet long! *Note:* your ability to access Symphony's spreadsheet depends on the RAM memory of your computer. It would take a RAM memory of over two million bytes to access all of the sheet.

With such a big spreadsheet, it is probably obvious that you won't be able to see all of it at one time. In fact, when you turn Symphony on and get into a SHEET environment, you are only looking at a small part of it. You see eight columns across, by 20 rows deep, or 160 cells. Compared to the total number of cells in the sheet, you're only seeing about .0076 percent of the whole. It's as if you are looking through a tiny window at the upper left corner of the sheet. (This may be all that some people will need to work with. Most, however, will use much more of Symphony's capabilities.) You can see the "tiny window" in Figure 4.2.

Since the view is like looking at only a small part of a landscape through a tiny window, you might wonder how you see the rest of the landscape? Or, how you see the rest of the spreadsheet? The answer is that you can move the "window" to other parts of the sheet.

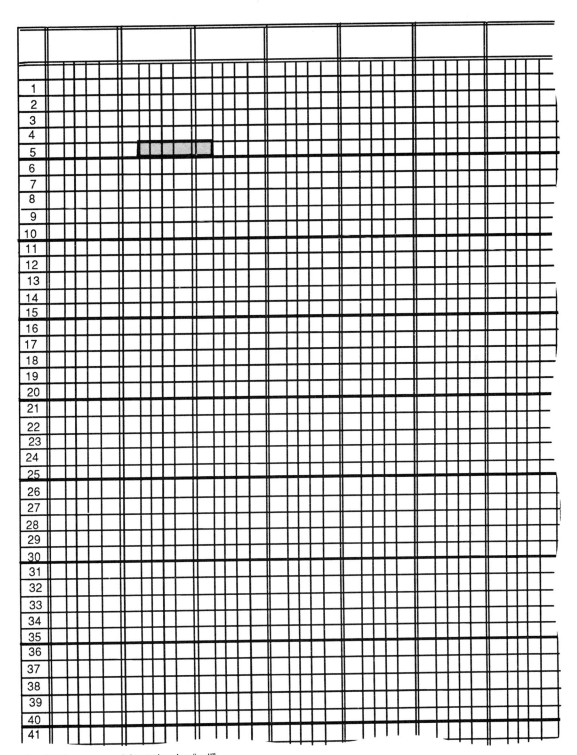

Fig. 4.1 Paper spreadsheet showing "cell".

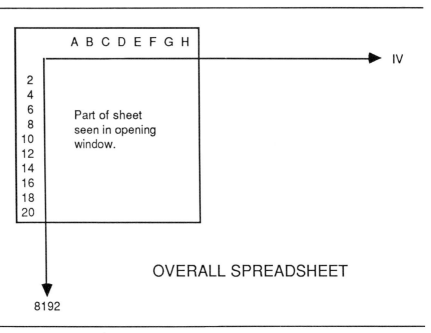

Fig. 4.2 Overall sheet showing the part seen in the opening window.

Furthermore, what makes Symphony so useful is that the screen can be split so that both parts of the spreadsheet can be seen at the same time. One window could be created in the first location for one part of your business and a different window created in the second. Then you could switch back and forth between windows, or have both windows displayed at the same time. In fact, as we'll see in a later chapter, there are almost no limitations to the number of windows that can be created with Symphony.

Limitations of Your Computer's Memory

Although Symphony has many, many cells, you cannot put information in every one of them. This is because Symphony keeps track of the entries you make in your computer's internal RAM memory. Thus, the number of entries you can make depends on the size of your computer's RAM. This can be critical to running the program.

Symphony requires a *minimum of 320K* in RAM *just to load*. If that is the maximum capacity of your computer, then after loading you will only have about 20K of RAM left for making entries. That's the equivalent of about one percent of Symphony's spreadsheet!

Of course, that may be more than enough for your needs. This book was written with Symphony's word processor capability on an IBM computer with 512K RAM. After loading the program, there remained approximately 212K RAM for writing, or the equivalent of about 100 pages, which is another way of thinking of Symphony's size.

To see what the available memory is in your computer, when in Symphony, hit

[**SERVICES**] ([**F9**] and then the SETTINGS selection from the menu. The first item in the settings display will be *available memory*. It will tell you how much you have, how much you've used, and what percent is left for use.

Potential Memory

One last point needs to be made with regard to memory. When we speak of the full size of Symphony's spreadsheet, we are talking of *potential*. It's most unlikely you'd ever use that much space.

What you do use can be considered Symphony's actual size for you. This has some interesting consequences. If you begin by putting the letter A in the cell in the first column and first row (most upper left), you will have used only one cell of the spreadsheet. However, if you put the letter A in the J column (10 columns over) in the 100th row, you will be using 1,000 of Symphony's cells. Roughly speaking, Symphony will only need a few bytes of memory to accommodate the first entry, but for the same letter A used lower in the spreadsheet, it will require over 1,000 bytes. In other words, even if you don't make entries in each cell, just by passing over them to make entries in further cells can use up memory. Therefore, I try to stick as close to the upper left of my sheet as possible for most work. Normally, there is more than enough space there. In Figure 4.3 you can see the changes in memory requirements.

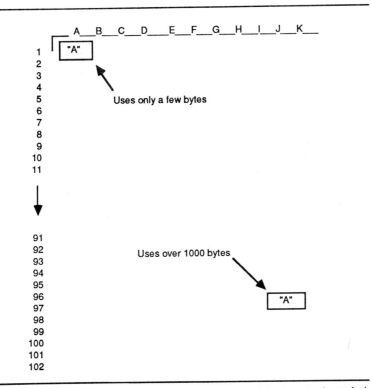

Fig. 4.3 Diagram showing 1 byte for corner cell, 1,000 bytes for lower cell. Make in the form of a lattice pattern.

Now that we have some appreciation for what Symphony's spreadsheet does and what it looks like, let's get started using it.

Opening a Spreadsheet

Perhaps the easiest of all tasks on Symphony is opening a spreadsheet. Simply call up Symphony (either by using the ACCESS program, or by typing "Symphony" (plus any version you may be using) after the A > prompt. You are immediately in a spreadsheet. If you are already in another mode, then simply "switch" [ALT] + [F10]. The MAIN MENU will give you five alternatives. Select SHEET and you'll be off and running.

Identify the Parts of the Spreadsheet

The spreadsheet that Symphony opens for you is huge. As you can quickly see, it is designed like a graph, with both a vertical and horizontal axis. The line along the top is divided by letters. Each letter represents a vertical column. The line along the side is divided by numbers. Each number represents a horizontal row. The point at which each letter column and row number cross on the spreadsheet is a *cell*. For example, cell number B5 is across one column, and down five rows.

Moving the Opening Window

As noted, with such a big spreadsheet, it really isn't possible to see all of it at one time; we can only see eight columns across by 20 columns deep, or 160 cells. As I said, we are looking through a tiny window at the upper left corner of the sheet.

So how do you see the rest of the landscape? How do you move the window?

Moving the Pointer to Move the Window

Recall that when you turned on Symphony, cell A1 was highlighted. The highlighted area on the screen is the spot where information can be entered. We'll do that in a moment, but for now, think of that highlighted area as a pointer to each cell in the window. Besides pointing at each cell, however, you can also ask the pointer to change the location of your window. For example, hit the [END] and [RIGHT ARROW]. Look at the top of the screen. The letters indicate that you have instantly been transported to the far right of the top 20 rows of the spreadsheet. Now hit [END] and [DOWN ARROW]. Look at the left edge of the screen. Instantly you have been transported to the bottom right corner of the spreadsheet.

Now hit [HOME]. You are back where you started. It is important to understand, however, that it is not the spreadsheet that is moving. The sheet remains in one spot. It is the window that scampers over the surface to different locations. This is a concept we'll use later when we open more than one window. We'll be able to divide up the screen to see different parts of the spreadsheet, and work in different windows at the same time.

Task — Move pointer
Command — ARROW KEYS
Explanation — There are a number of ways to move the pointer. The easiest way is to simply use the arrow keys on the keyboard. Hit the appropriate arrow key to move the pointer one cell (hold down for repeat movement).

Task — Rapid pointer movement
Command — ARROW KEY PLUS CONTROL
Explanation — For faster movement (covering more ground), hold [**CONTROL**] while hitting a [**LEFT**] or [**RIGHT ARROW**]. This moves the pointer *one full screen* right or left. Lotus calls this BIG RIGHT or BIG LEFT.

Task — Move pointer up or down
Command — UP OR DOWN ARROW KEYS
Explanation — Use the arrow keys to move the pointer *one row* up or down at a time. Hold down the arrow keys for repeat movement.

Task — Move screen up or down
Command — SCREEN UP OR DOWN/ARROW KEYS PLUS SCROLL LOCK KEY
Explanation — To move *one full screen* up or down (20 rows from where the pointer is) use [**PAGE UP**] or [**PAGE DOWN**]. To move *one row* at a time up or down, lock the pointer into place by hitting the [**SCROLL**] key. The arrow keys will now move the window, instead of just moving the pointer. For continuous scrolling up or down keep the arrow keys depressed.

Working in the Sheet

Task — Move quickly to distant parts of the spreadsheet
Command — END KEY PLUS ARROW KEY
Explanation — In addition, as we saw a few paragraphs ago, you can quickly jump to the far reaches of the spreadsheet, using [**END**] plus the arrow keys or [**HOME**]. This takes you across empty cells to the next batch of occupied cells. (Since we had a totally empty sheet when we tried it, it took us to the furthest corners. If, however, we had typed something into cell P1 for example, and the pointer was on row one, when we hit [**END**] + [**RIGHT ARROW**], we would only have gone as far as cell P1.)

Task — Go to a particular cell
Command — GOTO KEY ([**F5**])
Explanation — Hit [**GOTO**] ([**F5**]). At the top of the screen you are asked what cell to go to. Name a cell. You will be instantly transported there.

Task — Return to the top left cell in the SPREADSHEET

Command — HOME KEY

Explanation — [**HOME**] will instantly take you back to the upper left of the spreadsheet. *Note*: in some cases you may "restrict" your window to only a certain portion of the spreadsheet. In that case [**HOME**] will return you to the upper most left portion of the restricted area.

Figure 4.4 shows the concept of a moving window.

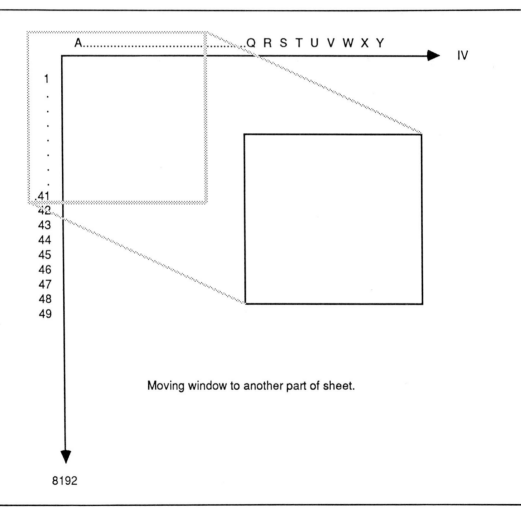

Moving window to another part of sheet.

Fig. 4.4 Concept of a moving window.

These, then, are the basic movements around a spreadsheet. Try them out a few times to get the feel of it. They aren't hard to use, and after awhile they will seem like old friends.

Now that you know your way around, it's time to get started making a few entries. There are essentially three types of cell entries — labels (text), numbers and formulas. We'll handle each separately.

Task — Enter a label in a cell
Command — WRITE IN LABEL WHEN POINTER IS ON CELL
Explanation — Words or letters are called *labels* in Symphony's vernacular. They usually refer to the titles or headings of charts you're working on. To enter a label, simply aim the pointer at any cell and type in whatever you want. Your label can be up to 240 characters long. (If it is longer than the space available in the cell, it will overlap an empty cell to the right. If the cell to the right is filled, Symphony will abbreviate the label.)

As you type, look up at the entry panel in the upper left of your screen. You should see the following:

A1:
FIRST

As you write out the label, what you've written appears on the second line of the screen. Now hit [**RETURN**]. This enters the label into the cell. *Moving the pointer to another location will also enter the label.*

Task — Change the location of the label within the cell
Command — PREFIXES
Explanation — Enter the word FIRST in any cell. When you've finished, you should now see FIRST in the cell, as well as the following in the entry top line:

A1: 'FIRST

Notice the apostrophe ' before the word. It appeared there even though you didn't enter it. It is a code prefix, which Symphony uses to help identify the placement of a label within a cell. It stands for *flush left*. The label is entered in the left side of the cell.

Symphony's prefixes for placing labels in sheet cells are:

' = Flush left   " = Flush right

^ = Centered

\ = Repeating (Repeats label in cell)

The default setting is normally the apostrophe, or *flush left*. Try rewriting the word, this time using the quotation sign ("FIRST). As you rewrite, the new entry replaces the old, and it will be flush right when you enter it into the cell.

Task — Change an entry
Command — RETYPE, OR EDIT
Explanation — The simplest way to change an entry you've made in a cell, is to aim the pointer at it, then type the new version. The old version will instantly disappear as the new one replaces it.

There is at least one drawback to this method. The old version is completely erased and you have to type in a completely new one. Sometimes it's easier to just correct a single letter. This can be accomplished using the EDIT key [**F2**]. Simply tap [**F2**] while your pointer is aimed at a cell in which you want to change an entry. You'll see EDIT appear in the upper right hand corner of your screen.

Now use the arrow keys to move the cursor to the part of the label you want to change. [**DELETE**] can be used to erase incorrect or unwanted characters which are *directly over the cursor*. [**BACKSPACE**] can be used to erase characters which are *directly to the left of the cursor*. Once an incorrect character has been removed, type in the right one.

Task — Enter a number (value) in a cell
Command — ENTER NUMBER
Explanation — Aim the pointer at the cell and type in the number. It will appear on the entry line at the upper left. Hitting [**RETURN**], or an arrow key, will enter the number into the cell.

Caution: you cannot enter commas or dollar signs when you enter a number. A decimal is always assumed if you don't enter it.

Task — Add dollar signs and commas to numbered entries (may also be used to add percentage signs, scientific notation and other items)
Command — SHEET, MENU, SETTINGS, FORMAT, CURRENCY
Explanation — To add dollar signs or commas, you must use the MAIN MENU [**F10**]. When the MENU appears, select the heading SETTINGS by pressing the S key, or aiming the pointer and using [**RETURN**].

When the SETTINGS MENU appears, select FORMAT. The FORMAT MENU (Figure 4.5) will appear.

```
Currency format specified on Configuration sheet                    MENU
Currency  Punctuated  Fixed  %  General  Date  Time  Scientific  Other
```

Fig. 4.5 The Format Menu.

You'll see that the pointer is aimed at CURRENCY. Simply hit [**RETURN**] to select it. You will now be asked how many decimal places you want. You may enter your choice (2 is the default). Finally, Symphony asks for the range you want to format. It is asking which cells the dollar sign should appear in. You will be returned to the sheet.

Just use the arrow keys to highlight the cells. (If you have trouble, see Chapter 5 on ranges.)

When you use [QUIT] or [ESC] to return to the sheet, you will see that both dollar signs and commas have been entered in the appropriate locations.

Note: don't panic if you see a row of asterisks where the numbers should be. Symphony is simply telling you that the number is too large to display. You can display the number by increasing the width of the column you are in.

Task — Increase column width
Command — SHEET, MENU, WIDTH
Explanation — You can increase the width of any single column, or all the columns in your window.

To change the size of a *single column*, first place the pointer in the column to be changed. Next, use the WIDTH command. You will be given the option of *setting* or *restoring*. Select *set*. The default will be shown as 9 spaces. You may change the number. When you finish, the column will be the width you want it to be.

To change the size of *all* the columns in a spreadsheet, use MENU, SETTINGS, WIDTH. You can now specify the width that you want all of the columns to be. *Note:* you can either type in the new width in numbers, or indicate it with the arrow keys.

Task — Copy a cell
Command — SHEET, MENU, COPY
Explanation — Copying the contents of a cell to one or more cells is very easy with Symphony (and similar to the procedure used in a DOC). Begin by calling up the MENU [F10]. The highlighted selection on the MENU will automatically be COPY. Simply hit C for COPY, or [RETURN]. The MENU will disappear and in its place will appear:

Copy FROM What Block?   A1. .A1

Symphony is asking what you want copied. You may specify *either* a single cell, or a range of cells. In the illustration above, the cell A1 is displayed as the default. Symphony will display whatever cell the pointer is aimed at as the default.

If you want to copy from one cell, highlight the cell with the pointer and hit [RETURN].

If you want to copy a range of cells, you must first define the range. "Range" simply means a group of cells. (See Chapter 5 on ranges for a further explanation.) You can see an example of this range of cells in Figure 4.6.

After you've hit [COPY], extend the range you want by using the arrow keys. You can move up, down, right or left. Whichever direction you move will be highlighted. *Note:* the highlighting indicates the *range* of cells to be copied. (See the chapter on ranges for highlighting techniques, including moving the anchor.)

After you've highlighted the cells to be copied, hit [RETURN]. A new message will now appear.

Range To Copy TO: A1

```
B3:                                                                        SHEET

---------A---------B---------C---------D---------E---------F-------G-------H-----┐
  1
  2
  3           ┌─────────────┐
  4           │    12       │
  5           │   234       │
              │    49       │
  6           │    57       │
  7           │    12       │
  8           │   356       │
  9           │   234       │
 10           │    33       │
 11           │   234       │
 12           │   792       │
 13           │    77       │
 14           │     3       │
 15           │    56       │
              └─────────────┘
 16
 17
 18
 19
 20 _____

15-Jun-85   01:38 PM
```

Fig. 4.6 Diagram showing a range of cells from the pointer.

The default will be the cell the pointer is aimed at. Using the arrow keys, you may now move the pointer to any cell on the sheet (or you can type in a cell location.) As soon as you hit [**RETURN**], the cell or the range you've indicated will be copied.

Task — Move a cell or range of cells
Command — SHEET, MENU, MOVE
Explanation — The procedure is identical to that for copying, explained above. With COPY, however, a duplicate of the original is created. With MOVE, the contents change location.

Task — Erase a cell or range of cells
Command — SHEET, MENU, ERASE
Explanation — Use the ERASE selection found from the SHEET MENU [**F10**]. The procedure is identical to that for copying, explained above. With ERASE, however, there is only one step—identifying the range. Once that is done, the first [**RETURN**] erases that cell or range.

These, then, are our basic movements in and around a spreadsheet. It isn't necessary to memorize them immediately. Just remember this chapter and refer back to it when you have a particular task you want to accomplish. Soon you'll find you can do it without even thinking about it.

Integrating a Document with a Sheet

We've now had a look at both a DOCUMENT and a SHEET environment. At this point you're probably wondering how to integrate the two.

As we go through the book, we'll see instances of integration, but for now, let's establish some basics:

Basics of Integrating

1. A DOCUMENT environment writes each line as an extended label in column A of the sheet.

2. If you move a document to a SHEET environment, it will all be in column A, regardless of how wide the text may be.

3. You can move a sheet (a range of columns and rows) into a blank area in a document. But these will usually occupy cells *other than those in column A*. Hence, in order to edit material moved from a sheet into a document, you will need to use the SHEET mode.

4. You can edit data moved into a document, provided it all goes into the A column. (This is also the case with a data form created by Symphony, as we'll see in later chapters.)

In conclusion, if you move text from a sheet into a document, and find you are having trouble editing, "switch" to the SHEET environment and try editing it using the EDIT ([**F2**]) command.

CHAPTER 5

Using Ranges

Thus far we have been talking about individual "cells," their location and how to utilize them. However, very often we are not concerned with a single cell, but with a group of cells. For example, we might create a row of values A2. .H2. The whole row would be called a *range* (Figure 5.1).

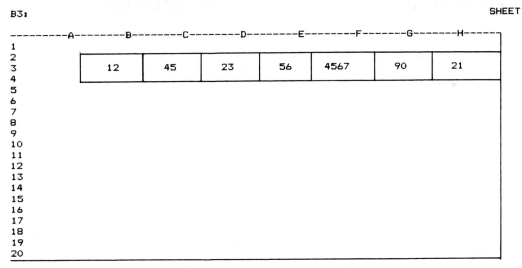

Fig. 5.1 Example of Horizontal Range (Single Row).

In the above case, the row represents the inventory at a business' downtown warehouse. But suppose a manager wanted to look at inventory stored in several warehouses. This might be a *vertical column range*, defined as B2. .B12 (Figure 5.2).

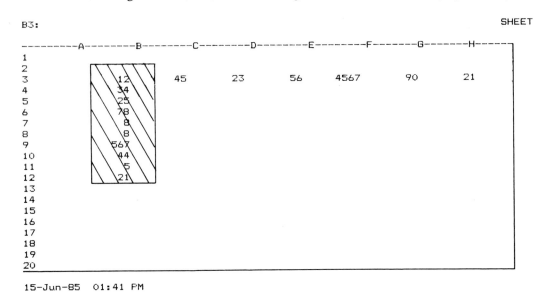

Fig. 5.2 Example of Vertical Range (Column).

In other words, a *range* simply means a *group of cells linked together*. Notice that it is defined by the two cells at its furthest edges. In the first case this was A2 to H2. In the second case it was B2 to B12.

Notice also the form that Symphony uses to indicate a range. It *always* requires two dots between the edge of the range cells. Not B1 to B5, not B1 — B5, but B1. .B5. (We can insert as many dots as we like between the defining cells, but Symphony will always replace them with just two.) In Figure 5.3 you can see the range written in the upper left hand corner.

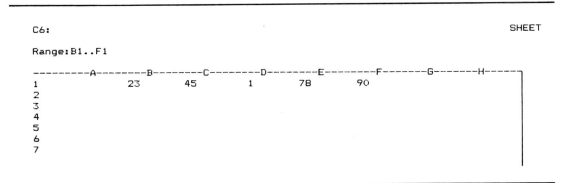

Fig. 5.3 Illustration showing range in upper left corner of screen.

Since a range of cells must always be identified by its two furthest cells, the range can only have two shapes, either a square or a rectangle. (The range can't turn or define angles.) This is illustrated in Figure 5.4.

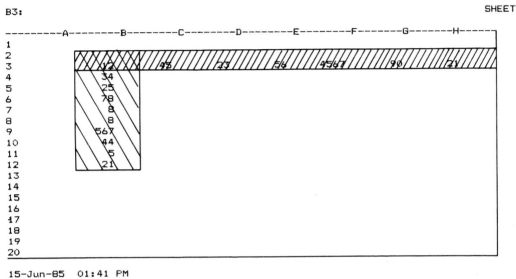

Fig. 5.4 Square and Rectangle (only two shapes possible) superimposed over sheet showing defining cells.

Ranges have a multitude of uses in Symphony, and we must understand them to get the most out of the program. For example, to print out a sheet, you must tell the printer the range you want printed. To create a graph, you must indicate the cells within a range to be graphed. Also, before you can move or manage a column, you must define it as a range. As noted, ranges are critical to understanding Symphony.

Defining a Range

Task — Define a range with arrow keys
Command — ARROW KEYS
Explanation — Many of Symphony's commands require that you define a range. For example, let's say you want to copy a column of numbers to a different location. As soon as you hit the copy command, SHEET, MENU, COPY, you will be asked, "Range To Copy From?" and the single cell location of your pointer will be indicated.

You can now anchor the pointer (see instructions below on anchoring), if it isn't already anchored, and "drag" the pointer from it's starting cell location across a range of cells. The range will become highlighted and the defining cells will be indicated at the upper left of your screen. You will have defined the range to be copied. (The copy procedure itself is defined elsewhere in this book.)

Task — Anchor the pointer
Command — TAB KEY OR PERIOD ([.])
Explanation — To anchor the pointer (or cursor) to keep it from hopping from cell to cell, or location to location, when you are defining a range, you can use either **[TAB]** or the period ([.], depending on the environment you are in. When you hit one of these keys, it tells the pointer that the cell you are on is the anchor, or the first defining cell, of your range. Now you may use the arrow keys to highlight any rectangular area.

Task — Release the anchored pointer
Command — ESCAPE KEY
Explanation — To release an anchored cell, hit **[ESC]**. You can change the anchor position within a range when defining a window by using the [.]. See Chapter 8 on windowing for a further explanation.

Task — Define a range by cell location
Command — Give defining cell numbers
Explanation — Instead of pointing out a range using the arrow keys, you can some-times type it in. All you need to do is to write the locations of defining cells (the cells at the two extremes of the range), placing two dots in between. Symphony will immedi-ately understand what you're instructing.

Naming a Range

Task — Name a range
Command — SHEET, MENU, RANGE, NAME, CREATE
Explanation — Symphony allows you to give any range a name. This is extremely useful when you want to go back and refer to the range at a later time. It also makes it easier to both recall and find a range. For example, which is easier to remember—a range called E32. .F37, or a range called SALESTOTALS?

Furthermore, Symphony allows you to name ranges quickly and easily. With the above commands, you are asked to write in the name of the range. Any identifying name will do, as long as it isn't more than 15 characters long.

Next, you are asked to identify the range. This can be done with the arrow keys.

Now you have a range with a name. Later on, for example, you can use the GOTO key **[F5]** and the range name (SALESTOTALS, in this case), to immediately go back to that range. We'll see many other uses as we go through the next chapters. *Note*: you can use a range in any of Symphony's environments, but you must use the SHEET to create a name.

Task — Determine what range names are in existence
Command — SHEET, RANGE, NAME, CREATE
Command — SHEET, RANGE, NAME, TABLE
Explanation — You can only use a name range once. Sometimes it's hard to remember

what names you have already used. (If you use a name a second time, the range values used first will be erased and replaced by the new range values that you enter—something you probably don't want to have happen.) There are two ways to see what names are currently in use. You can issue the CREATE command. Symphony will then provide a listing of all current range names and ask if you want to name a new one. Just use [ESC] several times to exit the command if you don't want to create a new name.

You can also use the TABLE command to create a table which includes all of the names in the current worksheet. You will be asked where you want the table to be located. Pick some convenient spot that is out of your current work range. Symphony will immediately create a table directory that includes the location of the cells to which the names refer.

Working with Range Names

Task — Delete a range name
Command — SHEET, RANGE, NAME, DELETE
Explanation — After issuing the above command, just point to the range name you want deleted and ENTER.

Task — Name a range with the labels adjacent to it
Command — SHEET, RANGE, NAME, LABELS
Explanation — This can be used to create range names, but *only* for labels existing in cells adjacent to their ranges. First, place the pointer on the cell containing the first label. Then follow the directions which come on the screen. They will indicate the direction of the adjacent cells that are to be included in the range. Then give the range.

Task — Eliminate all the range names in the current spreadsheet
Command — SHEET, MENU, NAME, RESET
Explanation — This deletes *all* the names at once.

Changing Ranges

Task — Copy a row range into a column range or vice versa
Command — SHEET, MENU, RANGE, TRANSPOSE
Explanation — This transposes vertical ranges with horizontal ranges. *Warning*: it is a dangerous command. Remember, the basis behind Symphony's spreadsheet is the *location* of cells. When transposing a range of formulas, you may significantly change locations, and formulas could produce results that are very different than anticipated.

This command first asks for the range to copy from, then the range to copy to. It does not just *move* a range, it *reproduces* it on a *different* plane. Notice that when copying or moving to a range, you need only give the cell location that is in the upper left hand corner, *not* the full range you are copying or moving to.

Task — Change a range of formulas into their values while copying.
Command — SHEET, MENU, RANGE, VALUE
Explanation — This is not as outlandish a command as it first may seem. You may have created a row of formulas. Now you want to see their current values expressed in a different location. If you indicate the current location as the place to move to, you can have the formulas transformed to their values without changing locations.

Task — Change the location of the labels within a range of cells
Command — SHEET, MENU, RANGE, LABEL-ALIGNMENT
Explanation — You can change the left, center or right alignment of a row of labels with this command. It *only* works on labels, not values.

Task — Create a group of evenly spaced numbers within a range
Command — SHEET, MENU, RANGE, FILL
Explanation — This is a shortcut command. Let's say you want to create a row with the numbers 5, 10, 15, 20, 25 and 30, in consecutive cells. This command can do it for you.
     As soon as you call up FILL, you are asked for a range. Specify as many cells as you want filled. Next you are asked for the first number. In this case it would be 5. Then you are asked for the interval. Since there are five numbers between the first (5), and the second (10), the interval is 5. Finally, you are asked how many cells to fill. Since you've already indicated six cells in the range, you can simply hit [**ENTER**] and the six will be filled. However, if you had only wanted the first three of the six filled, you could have specified 15.

Task — Find the distribution in a range of numbers
Command — SHEET, RANGE, DISTRIBUTION
Explanation — This is an extremely useful command, though at first it seems complex (it isn't). Suppose you want to break down the distribution of interest rates in a series of loans that you are holding in a portfolio. Your portfolio might look like this:

INTEREST RATES OF
DIFFERENT LOANS

11
12
11
8
14
12
9
10
14
11
13
10

You might want to know how many loans you're holding with an interest rate of 9 percent, how many at 10, at 11, at 12 percent and so forth. This command will give you the distribution.

First, you need the data to be distributed (shown above). Next, you need the frequency range, to be provided in a *bin*. This is how the distribution is to be arranged. Here we simply want it arranged by percentages, such as shown under BIN below:

	A	**B**	**C**
1	LOAN RATES	BIN	DISTRIBUTION
2	11	8	1
3	12	9	1
4	11	10	2
5	8	11	3
6	14	12	2
7	12	13	1
8	9	14	2
9	10		0
10	14		
11	11		
12	13		
12	10		

(The BIN column can be filled in by using the FILL command.) When you issue the distribution command, you will first be asked the data range (B1. .B12). Next you'll be asked the bin range (F1. .F8). After this Symphony will quickly calculate the distribution, shown in the above table at right. It tells you how many loans fall into each category (how many are between 9 and 10, how many between 10 and 11, and so forth).

Note: the bin range must always be a vertical column, and it must always be in *ascending* order (the smallest number at the top).

CHAPTER
6

Getting Started
With Formulas

The usefulness of any spreadsheet lies in its formulas. However, you don't have to be a mathematical wizard to use formulas in a sheet. In fact, you don't have to know much math at all. What is required, instead, is a clear understanding of what you want to accomplish. After all, your purpose in creating a spreadsheet is to help you solve a particular problem, not to show off your mastery of mathematics.

Here's an example of the sort of problem you might want to solve or find alternate solutions to, using the worksheet:

Problem: A sales organization has seven salespeople. The manager has access to the following information:

PERSON	SALES	PERSON	SALES
John	$1,300	Dorothy	$1,900
Helen	$1,750	Pete	$4,300
Marty	$3,100	Willard	$1,800
Ellen	$1,275		

The manager wants to know the following on a weekly basis:

1. The dollar commission paid to each salesperson (@20% of sales).

2. The total amount of all sales.

3. The total commissions paid.

4. The percentage of sales that each person is contributing.

The manager wants to know this information in order to determine what volume of business the company is producing, what the commission expenses are and who the best producers are.

Keep in mind that the manager could figure out all of this information each week using a calculator and several sheets of paper. However, it is much easier to use an electronic spreadsheet.

Spreadsheet solution: to solve the above problem on a sheet requires three different kinds of data:

*   Labels — (names of salespeople, items covered, etc.)

*   Values — (input of sales amounts and commissions paid)

*   Formula — (relationships of data and labels)

To get what he wants, the manager must create a worksheet that incorporates all of the information he has. He must also create a worksheet that provides a clear understanding of how all the information is related.

Creating the Worksheet Format

The manager should begin with the labels (text). We've already covered the way labels are created in a worksheet (see the last chapter), so it should be possible to produce the following chart just by typing in the data:

	A	B	C	D
1	PERSON	SALES	COMMISSION	PERCENTAGE
2	John			
3	Helen			
4	Marty			
5	Ellen			
6	Dorothy			
7	Pete			
8	Willard			
	Totals			

Simply by moving the pointer to the appropriate cells and typing in the labels shown above, we can create a form that will take into account all the information that the manager wishes to know.

Adding the Values

Now that he has the labels, the manager's next step would be to add the values. We're presuming that he knows the sales each person is producing. These would be entered in the second column.

	A	B	C	D
1	PERSON	SALES	COMMISSION	PERCENTAGE
2	John	$1,300		
3	Helen	$1,750		
4	Marty	$3,100		
5	Ellen	$1,275		
6	Dorothy	$1,900		
7	Pete	$4,300		
8	Willard	$1,800		
	Totals			

The manager simply enters the gross sales, *without any dollar signs or commas*, after the name of each person. (Remember, to access dollar signs and commas, you use the **MENU -FORMAT -CURRENCY** format when in a spreadsheet.) So, now the labels and values have been entered. The remainder of this chart will be made up of formulas expressing the relationships the manager wants.

≣Entering Formulas

Task — Put a formula into a cell
Command — PLUS SIGN
Explanation — A formula can be entered in a cell just like a label or a value. However, the manager must first tell Symphony that it is dealing with a formula. The basic method of entering a formula is to first enter a plus sign " + ". This lets Symphony know that what follows will not be data (neither alphabetic nor numeric). After the plus sign, he may enter either numbers or cell locations (Figure 6.1).

Task — Define operators used in formulas
Command — +, −, *, /, <, >, =, ^
Explanation — Symphony understands the following basic operators:

Add (+) Subtract (−) 2 Multiply (*) Divide (/)

```
B3:                                                                    SHEET


--------A--------B--------C--------D--------E--------F-------G-------H-----┐
1
2
3                +1300*.2
4
5
6
7
8
9
10
11                                                                        │
```

Fig. 6.1 Illustration of Entering Formula.

In addition, these others may also be used:

< Less than
> Greater than
= Equal to
^ Raise to a higher power.

& And

If more than one operator is used in a formula, what is the order in which Symphony performs the operations? Generally speaking, the following order is used:

First —   &
Second —   <, >, =
Third —   +, −
Fourth —   * /
Fifth —   ^

Note: +, − can also mean positive and negative, in which case their order of preference would come just before exponentiation [^].)

For clarity, parentheses () may also be added to formulas.

Task — Create a formula
Explanation — Let's use an example to illustrate this, namely the commission formula for the model spreadsheet created above.

The Commission Formula

Our manager knows that each person's commission is 20 percent of the sales produced. What he needs to do, therefore, is to express this in a formula. Let's begin with the first salesperson, John. John's sales for the week are $1,300. His commission is 20 percent of that. What would a simple formula for this look like?

The manager would take the amount earned, $1,300, and multiply it by 20 percent. A simple formula to express this would be:

$1,300 * 20% = ?

Moving to cell B3, he would write in this formula:

+1300*.20

The percent is converted to a decimal. A plus sign is typed in, alerting Symphony to the fact that a formula is to follow. The amount of the commission is also typed in; then a multiplication sign (*). Finally, the percentage of the commission is added. If you do this on a worksheet, the answer, 260 in this case, will immediately pop up.

This works, but it has a drawback. Now when the manager moves down to calculate the commission for the next person (row C3 in the preceding examples), he will need to type in a new sales figure. In fact, he'll have to type in the sales figures for each person on the list. If he's going to do that, he might as well use a hand-held calculator.

A Better Method

Instead of typing in the amount of sales for each salesperson, the manager could create a different formula that more clearly expressed the relationship he wanted to define. This is not nearly as complicated as it sounds. What he wants to do is to take 20 percent *of the value in the cell to the left* for each row. Here is a simple formula that will do this:

TYPE INTO CELL C2 +b2*.20

Notice the difference here. Instead of the dollar amount, the cell location where the dollar amount is given is typed in.

Important Rule — Symphony formulas work on the basis of locations. All that's needed in a formula is to alert Symphony to the location of a cell and what you want done with the value in it.

In fact, the manager need not even *type* in B2. As soon as he types in the plus sign (+), letting Symphony know it's dealing with a formula, he can use the pointer to tell it which cell he is concerned with. To do this he just points at the cell he wants included, and hits [+] (or whatever operator applies).

Symphony immediately understands that it should add the value from the pointed cell to the formula being written. Now the pointer leaps back to the active cell, and Symphony is ready to add additional information.

Using cell locations, instead of typing in values, is far more efficient because the relationship it expresses may now be copied into other cells. In our example, the manager wants to set up the same relationship for Helen and the rest of the sales force that he used for John. Therefore, instead of rewriting formulas, all he needs to do is copy the formula for John's commission into the rows for the other salespeople. In other words, he simply *copies* the information contained in cell C2 into cells C3. .C8.

Task — Copy formula in C2 to C3. .C8
Command — SHEET, MENU, COPY
Explanation — Indicate that the cell to copy from is C2. .C2. Indicate that the range to copy to is C3. .C8. Hit [**RETURN**]. (If you're not sure how to do this, see the explanations in Chapters 4 and 5.)

The correct amount (20 percent of the sales amounts for each salesperson) will immediately appear in cells C3 to C8. This works because Symphony remembers relationships. When we copy cell C3, we copy the relationship, which can be expressed as: *multiply the cell on the left by 20%.*

	A	B	C	D
1	PERSON	SALES	COMMISSION	PERCENTAGE
2	John	$1,300	+B2*.20	
3	Helen	$1,750	+B3*.20	
4	Marty	$3,100	+B4*.20	
5	Ellen	$1,275	+B5*.20	
6	Dorothy	$1,900	+B6*.20	
7	Pete	$4,300	+B7*.20	
8	Willard	$1,800	+B8*.20	
9				
10	Totals			

Symphony does this all the way down the row and the manager ends up with the correct sales commissions.

	A	B	C	D
1	PERSON	SALES	COMMISSION	PERCENTAGE
2	John	$1,300	$260	
3	Helen	$1,750	$350	
4	Marty	$3,100	$620	
5	Ellen	$1,275	$255	
6	Dorothy	$1,900	$380	
7	Pete	$4,300	$860	
8	Willard	$1,800	$360	
9				
10	Totals			

The Sales Total Formula

Next, the manager will likely want to calculate the sales total. The total will go into cell B10. He would move the pointer to that cell. For the formula, he needs to add up all the amounts in column B. The easiest way to do this is to simply enter in a string of additions:

FOR CELL B10
+ B2 + B3 + B4 + B5 + B6 + B7 + B8

When he locks this formula into cell B10 (by hitting [**RETURN**] or an arrow key) the sum of all the numbers above will appear, and he will have his sales total.

The Commissions Total Formula

Now he needs to get the commissions total. He could use the same formula as above. However, there is a method that seems a bit more complicated, yet is far easier to use. The method involves *functions*, which are a kind of shorthand. They can express, in only a few characters, what would otherwise be a very long formula. We'll learn a great deal more about functions in the next chapter, but for now, let's look at the function that handles addition of a group of numbers in a string.

Task — Use a function to *sum* numbers
Command — "@SUM"
Explanation — The manager could just write as follows, "@SUM (C2. .C8)". It means the same thing as the formula used for adding the sales total:

@SUM(C2. .C8) = + C2 + C3 + C4 + C5 + C6 + C7 + C8

Note that he does not need to use a plus sign to introduce the function. The @ sign tells Symphony that he is in a formula. Now **@SUM(C2. .C8)** just needs to be entered into cell C10.

At this point, the manager has the commissions and the totals for sales and commission. The sheet should look like this:

	A	B	C	D
1	PERSON	SALES	COMMISSION	PERCENTAGE
2	John	$1,300	$260	
3	Helen	$1,750	$350	
4	Marty	$3,100	$620	
5	Ellen	$1,275	$255	
6	Dorothy	$1,900	$380	
7	Pete	$4,300	$860	
8	Willard	$1,800	$360	
10	Totals	$15,425	$3,085	

The Formula for Percentage of Sales

Finally, in his analysis, the manager wants to find out the percentage of sales each salesperson contributed. To do this, yet another formula is needed, for percentages.

To find the percentage of something, you create a fraction, and then divide the denominator (bottom) into the numerator (top). In this case, the manager starts with the first salesperson. John sold $1,300, out of total sales of $15,425. As a fraction, his effort is:

$$\frac{1,300}{15,425.}$$

The solution to this fraction should appear in cell D2. To accomplish this, he must first go to cell D2. Then he must create a formula to express this fraction. How does he determine the formula? One way is by writing the fraction into the cell, using the cell locations. In other words, value 1,300 is in cell B2, and value 15,425 is in cell B10, so we end up with the formula:

+B2/B10

This is a simple expression of the same fraction we discussed earlier. Dividing the total sales into John's share yield's a percentage, which is expressed as the decimal .0843. Later we'll convert this to a percentage, using the MENU, FORMAT, PERCENT-AGE command. Then we'll see more clearly that it's 8.43%.

A Problem

The formula we've been working with is for cell D2. Now what about cell D3? Recalling what we've learned, you might think that the manager could now simply copy the formula from D2 into D3, D4, and so on down the column. Unfortunately, things won't work that way. What this formula says, according to Symphony is:

(Formula in cell D2) +B2/B10 = divide the second cell in the second column to the left, by the tenth cell in the second column to the left.

Can you see the problem? In this formulation we are asking Symphony to consider two cells. One is always two columns to the left. The other is always nine cells down, two columns to the left. That works out fine for the cell two columns to the left, since as you go down the rows, this always places the sales figures for the next salesperson in your formula.

But when you consider the cell nine cells down and two columns to the left, you find that it doesn't always contain the total sales figure! This is because the total sales figure is *always* in the same cell, in this example, cell B10. But the formula looks one cell lower with each calculation. (Remember, it's looking for the cell nine cells down and two to the left, *not* cell B10.)

The Solution

The solution, then, is that you don't want the position of the second cell in your formula to be *relative* (can change), but to be *absolute*. Regardless of what cell the calculation is made from, you always want it to calculate the denominator as B10. In fact, in any similar formula, the numerator in the equation is a relative cell, the denominator must be an absolute cell. How then do you make a cell reference absolute?

Making a Cell Reference Absolute

The manager could start off the formula as before +B2/. This establishes the cell two to the left, as a relative position.

Now, however, instead of typing in C10, which would also be a relative reference to Symphony, the manager could type in the *code for absolute*. (Symphony interprets the dollar sign to mean that a cell is to remain absolute, regardless of where the formula may be positioned. Each calculation is to be made with the same cell, in this case, C10).

Symphony provides a simple way of accomplishing this. After the first part of the formula is entered, the manager now aims the pointer at cell C10 (the commissions total). Then he hits the (Absolute) key **[F3]**. This locks in cell C10 as absolute. It also adds a dollar sign to the cell so that he will know it's absolute. The formula now reads:

FORMULA FOR CELL D2
+B2/C10

As soon as he hits **[RETURN]**, the correct percentage will appear in cell D2. He can now copy D2 to the range D3 — D8, and all the correct percentages will immediately appear (as decimals, of course).

Finally, using the FORMAT MENU, reached from the MAIN MENU, he can select the % option. The decimals will instantly be converted to percentages. The final chart will look like:

	A	B	C	D
1	PERSON	SALES	COMMISSION	PERCENTAGE
2	John	$ 1,300	$260	8%
3	Helen	$ 1,750	$350	11%
4	Marty	$ 3,100	$620	20%
5	Ellen	$ 1,275	$255	8%
6	Dorothy	$ 1,900	$380	12%
7	Pete	$ 4,300	$860	28%
8	Willard	$ 1,800	$360	12%
9				
10	Totals	$15,425	$3,085	100%

Spreadsheet Power

Now that we've traced the steps to creating our first small spreadsheet, it's important that we don't overlook the power it has. In addition to making various calculations, Symphony also does *automatic recalculation*.

This means that every time you change an entry in the spreadsheet, Symphony recalculates for you. If you've created a spreadsheet in your computer as described in this book, try changing an entry. For example, under John's sales, change the amount from $1,300 to $1,400.

As you enter this, watch what happens to John's commission, the sales and commissions totals, and all of the percentages. They are all changed automatically to accommodate the one small change you made! That's the power of Symphony.

As a further application, Symphony allows us to play "What if" games with the spreadsheet. For example, you might want to know what would happen if John's sales equalled those of Pete, the top salesperson? How much would the totals increase and what would the increase do to the overall percentages? You can type in Pete's $4,300, and Symphony will immediately recalculate to showing you.

"What if" tables also calculate a broad spectrum of possibilities.

A What If? Table

Task — Build a "What If" table
Command — SHEET, MENU, RANGE, WHAT IF
Explanation — A "What if" table is used to test a series of data against a formula. The best way of understanding this is to look at an example.

Suppose you are in business and want to know what your advertising budget should be for the next year. You are planning to spend X amount of dollars, and want X to be equal to a set percentage of your income. However, you don't know what your income will actually be.

Therefore, what you really want is a series of amounts that you might spend, depending on what your company's income turns out to be. Here is a breakdown of potential income over the next fiscal year:

INCOME

	A	B	C	D
1				
2				
3	$750,000			
4	$800,000			
5	$850,000			
6	$900,000			
7	$950,000			

You know that you want to spend 10 percent of income for advertising. In addition, regardless of what you spend, you have a $20,000 annual retainer at an advertising agency, that is over and above any advertising. Therefore, you come up with a formula for advertising that is $20,000, plus 10 percent of income, or D1 plus (D2*.1), assuming that cell D1 contains the amount $20,000, and that cell D2 contains the yearly income. Now enter the information you have on the rest of your sheet:

	A	B	C	D
1				$20,000
2		FORMULA		INPUT CELL
3	$750,000			
4	$800,000			
5	$850,000			
6	$900,000			
7	$950,000			

Notice that the first column lists potential income. This is your data list. Take note also that FORMULA is entered in cell B2. This is called the *master formula*. It will do all the calculations. The master formula is located one cell up and one cell to the right of your data list.

The *reference cell* (D1) contains a number which remains constant. It is located to the right. The *input cell* (D2) is an *empty* work cell where Symphony is going to do all its calculations.

Now call up the command: SHEET, MENU, RANGE, WHAT IF. The first question that appears asks whether you want a single or a double equation, or if you want to *reset*. Reset means that Symphony doesn't remember the location of previous table ranges. It's a good place to start because reset will take you back to the sheet again and you'll have to go through the commands to get to WHAT IF.

When you have reached WHAT IF, select the single equation. (We'll get to the double equation in a moment).

You are now asked the *data range*. This includes *both* the data list *and* the master formula. (See data list, indicated in the illustration above.) Next you are asked the input cell. (The cell where Symphony does all its calculations. It is indicated in the illustration above.) As soon as you're done, Symphony makes the calculation and enters the results in the column next to the one in which you put your data.

	A	B	C	D
1				$20,000
2		FORMULA		INPUT
3	$750,000	$ 95,000		
4	$800,000	$100,000		
5	$850,000	$105,000		
6	$900,000	$110,000		
7	$950,000	$115,000		

You now have a display of the cost of your advertising program based on five different WHAT IF income data.

Double Formula

A double formula uses two sets of variables. In the above illustration for example, you may want to know what the costs will be, not only for different incomes, but also for different percentages of advertising. Perhaps you want to know what the costs will look like if you invest 8%, 9%, 10%, 11%, or 12% of your income for advertising. The two variables you want to compare are income *and* advertising rate.

This time you need to create *two* data lists, one for income, and one for advertising rates. The first will be vertical, like the list above. The second will be horizontal. You will then see this:

	A	B	C	D	E	F
1	FORMULA	8%	9%	10%	11%	12%
2	$750,000					
3	$800,000					
4	$850,000					
5	$900,000					
6	$950,000					
7	20000					
8						

It's important to understand that you've created a "right angle," with the FORMULA at the corner. Now for the formula. It should be $20,000 (for the retainer), plus the percent variable times the income variable. For example:

+A7+(A8*B8)

where A7 is the constant $20,000, A8 is the income variable, and B8 is the commission rate variable. The input cells have been entered arbitrarily.

	A	B	C	D	E	F
1	FORMULA	8%	9%	10%	11%	12%
2	$750,000					
3	$800,000					
4	$850,000					
5	$900,000					
6	$950,000					
7	20000					
8	INPUT 1	INPUT 2				

Now your table is ready. Call up the WHAT IF command and select 2-WAY. For the table, indicate both the vertical and horizontal ranges (A1. .F6). You are now asked for *two* input cells. Indicate A8 and B8. After a few seconds the following chart should appear on your screen:

	A	B	C	D	E	F
1	FORMULA	8%	9%	10%	11%	12%
2	$750,000	$80,000	$ 87,500	$ 95,000	$102,500	$110,000
3	$800,000	$84,000	$ 92,000	$100,000	$108,000	$116,000
4	$850,000	$88,000	$ 96,500	$105,000	$113,500	$122,000
5	$900,000	$92,000	$101,000	$110,000	$119,000	$128,000
6	$950,000	$96,000	$105,500	$115,000	$124,500	$134,000
7	20000					
8	ENTRY 1	ENTRY 2				

Symphony has plotted every possible combination, since the incomes and advertising rate variables you have entered. *Note*: if Symphony takes some time to make the calculation, don't be alarmed. This is quite a bit of math, even for a computer!

Turning Off Recalculation

As we've seen, Symphony is constantly recalculating. Each time we make one entry, Symphony recalculates the sheet. But sometimes we don't want Symphony to do this. Recalculation takes time, particularly on a big spreadsheet. If we don't need an immediate recalculation, we can save the few seconds it requires by turning it off. That means turning recalculation from *automatic* to *manual*.

Task — Turn off recalculation
Command — SHEET, MENU, SETTINGS, RECALCULATION
Explanation — When you select RECALCULATION, you are presented with several choices. The first is between manual and automatic. The default is automatic, which means Symphony recalculates with each entry. You can select manual, however, and Symphony will only recalculate when you ask it to by pressing the CALC key [**F8**].

The next choice is between *order* and *natural* settings. The default is natural, which means that Symphony will make its first recalculations on the most basic cells in any formula, and only recalculate those cells on which these basic cells depend. In our example, it will calculate the individual commissions of the salespeople, before calculating the total commission.

In some cases, however, you may prefer to have Symphony recalculate row by row (from top to bottom), or column by column (from left to right). These options are given by selecting *order*.

Iteration refers to the number of times (1 to 50) that Symphony will attempt a recalculation. This is used in the case of a circular formula, where two cells depend on each other's solution. Usually, (but not always), this is an unintentional error. When you set Symphony to an iteration higher than 1, it will take some time to adjust. It will also indicate the location of the troublesome cells in the settings window.

Using Labels in Formulas

Thus far we have been entering only number values in our formulas. Symphony, however, allows us to also use labels in formulas, even though this seems beyond a computer's capability.

For example, we may have two labels in two different cells: "word" in one and "processing" in another. Symphony will allow us to combine these two to for "word-processing."

Symphony can accomplish some amazing feats with labels. A label is technically known as a *string*, meaning a string of individual characters. Symphony can search a cell to determine the length of the string of characters, and a character in a particular position in the string. It can also attach numerous strings together. In the next chapter we'll see that by using functions, Symphony can even change the characters in a string to make them all upper case or lower case, as well as perform other equally useful tasks.

Task — Join two or more literal strings together

Command — &

Explanation — Part of the key to the "stringing" together of words in a Symphony formula, is to identify the different elements. To accomplish this, you use a special operator, the ampersand "&". When you add an ampersand to a cell location in a formula, Symphony understands that you are talking about a label, and lets you manipulate the cell's string.

Consider the "Word processing" label again. We want to add the words WORD and PROCESSING together, even though they occur in different cells. Here's how to accomplish this: assume that WORD is in cell A1 and PROCESSING is in cell B2. You can join them together in a third cell by writing:

+A1&B2

The result will be:

WORDPROCESSING

A great many strings can be formed in this fashion. For example, +A1&B1&C1&D1&E1, up to the limit of the cell you are in (240 characters).

Task — Add spaces and/or words to a combined string

Command — " "

Explanation — While the use of the ampersand is obviously quite helpful, it can lead to problems. For example, let's say that instead of joining the two words, WORD and PROCESSING together, we wanted to join the words PETE and HARRY. Using the formula with ampersands only, as indicated above, we'd end up with PETEHARRY. But we wanted PETE and HARRY. How do we separate the two strings PETE, HARRY, and add the word AND between them?

The solution is to use quotation marks (" "). When you use quotation marks in a formula which also contains the ampersand, Symphony understands that anything between the quotation marks is to be added literally to the formula. For example, suppose you have PETE in cell A1, and HARRY in cell B2. You want to combine these strings, yet have them separated by a space, so that the words don't run together. Here's the formula, written into cell C3:

+A1&" "&B2

This yields:

PETE HARRY.

Notice the space left between the quotation marks. It was incorporated into the formula in order to leave an empty space between the two names. Notice also the positioning of the ampersand on the *outside* of the quotation marks. Let's try again:

+A1&"   AND   "&B2

This yields:

PETE AND HARRY

Notice that the area in quotes included a space, the word AND and another space.

With this process (called "concatenation"), you can manipulate labels. In the next chapter we'll see a group of special functions that can be used with strings to greatly increase our ability to handle labels.

Task — Change only a part of a formula in a cell
Command — EDIT KEY ([F2])
Explanation — We've already covered this task several times, but there's an added feature that needs to be mentioned. Sometimes you'll want to go back to a cell in which you've previously typed a label, values or a formula, in order to change only one part of it, not the whole. But if you simply start typing when you reach the cell, Symphony will erase everything that is in it, and you'll have to start from scratch.

On the other hand, if, when you get to the cell you want to work in, you hit the EDIT key ([F2], you'll find you can go back and selectively change any part of the cell that you want. The current contents are displayed on the edit line in the upper left of the screen. The arrow keys can be used to move the cursor under any part of the line. Then, either the [BACKSPACE] or [DELETE] is used to remove unwanted characters or values. Finally, you can selectively type in corrections.

Try the [F2] when you want to change or correct a previously created formula in a cell. It's marvelously easy!

Setting Goals

In this chapter we have gone through the procedure for creating a spreadsheet, using formulas. What is important to keep in mind is that the formulas we used were not standard formulas that were simply waiting in the wings to be used. Rather, we developed them to suit the material we were working with. The process involved determining relationships we wanted the cells in the spreadsheet to represent, and then expressing them in terms of notation that Symphony would understand. It's simply a matter of determining what you want to accomplish, and then putting those goals into a formulation that Symphony can interpret and act on.

Most people will probably never get beyond the basic operators (+ − / *), and one or two functions. Others may move further into Symphony for more complex and specific operations, which we'll cover in the next chapters. It's important to remember that what counts is not how much of Symphony you use, but that what you use accomplishes your goals.

CHAPTER
7

Advanced

Formulas

and Functions

Many Symphony users will find that they are able to get all they need out of the program just by creating simple formulas using the operators described in Chapter 6. However, as you learn more, you will find that one of the great benefits of Symphony, are the shortcuts it provides through the use of *functions*. The functions provide a quick and easy way to handle otherwise cumbersome and complex formulas. In some cases, the functions provide the only way to accomplish a task. While they may take a little getting used to, most functions are simple to use.

In this chapter we are going to take a close look at many of Symphony's functions. However, I want to point out that Symphony has over 75 functions! Most users will find that only a few of these are applicable to their work. The goal of this chapter is to provide a quick reference for all of Symphony's functions, while at the same time explaining in greater detail those most likely to be used.

The Parts of a Function Formula

The Function
There are essentially two parts to an advanced formula. One part is the *function* itself. In the last chapter we were introduced to one of Symphony's simplest functions, @SUM.

The Argument
The other part of an advanced function formula would be the *argument*. No, the argument doesn't involve computer keys combatting each other. It refers instead to the information the function operates *on*.

Typically, the argument is enclosed in parentheses. In the last chapter we used a formula that looked like this:

@SUM(B2. .B9)

The first part of the formula was the function. The second part, which contained a cell range reference, was the argument. An argument usually will contain a cell reference or specific numbers.

Function Rules

There are certain general rules by which functions operate. They include:

1. **You must put an @ symbol before the function name.**

2. **You can't leave empty spaces in a function formula.** (The exception is a string enclosed by quotation marks.)

3. **The argument should be enclosed by parentheses.**

4. With certain exceptions, the **functions are designed to operate on values**, not labels. (A label may end up being assigned the number value, 0.)

5. **You can have more than one function in a formula.** A function can be contained within parentheses and be part of the argument of another function, *or* it can be included with its own argument after another function. Here is a compound function formula:

@SUM(A1. .A10)*@SUM(B1. .B10)

(Multiply the sum of cells A1 to A10 by the sum of cells B1 to B10.)

Types of Symphony Functions

Symphony's functions are broken up into the following categories:

Mathematical Functions

Business Functions

Statistic Functions

Date and Time Functions

Database Functions

String Functions

True/False Functions

Look up Functions

Let's take a closer look at these functions, with the exception of the data base functions which are examined in the chapters concerning data base. We'll begin with the mathematical functions.

Mathematical Functions

Task — Find the sum of a range of numbers
Function — @SUM
Explanation — This is a simple adding function. For example, the formula +A1+A2+A3+A4+A5+A6+A7+A8+A9+A10, can be expressed by the function, @SUM(A1. .A10)

Task — Round off a decimal number
Function — @ROUND
Explanation — This function allows the user to round off a decimal. The user specifies how many decimal places are to be rounded off.

Two entries must be made in the argument. The first is the decimal number to be rounded; the second is the number of decimal places to be rounded off (up to 15 places, plus or minus). For example, let's say that we are dealing with British pounds, which are currently selling for 1.25789 pounds to the dollar. Working with five decimal places can be confusing. We could ask Symphony to round off this number to two decimal places, using this formula:

@ROUND(1.25789,2)

Notice the comma in the argument. It separates the number to be acted on, by the digits to be rounded off. (A similar operation is handled by the function @INT. @INT, however, simply transforms a number with a decimal to a number without one.)

Task — Find the absolute value of a number
Function — @ABS
Explanation — This function strips the minus signs off numbers in cells, to give the *absolute value*. (If there is a positive number in the cell, it will simply produce that number. If the cell is empty, it will produce a 0.) The form is:

@ABS(– 4567)

which yields:

4567

Task — Find the square root of a number
Function — @SQRT
Explanation — This function can be used to find the square root of any *positive* number. (It will not work for a negative number). The form is:

@SQRT(9)

which would yield 3.

Task — Find the sine, cosine, or tangent of a number
Function — @SIN, @COS, @TAN
Explanation — These are used when dealing with angles. They are expressed, however, in *radians*, instead of degrees. The radian is based on the mathematical pi (3.14159). Degrees can be converted to radians using the formula:

radians = degrees * @PI/180.

Task — Find the remainder of a fraction
Function — @MOD
Explanation — Frequently, when a fraction is divided, it will not come out even. For example, 9/4 (4 divided into 9), will result in 2 with 1 left over. The @MOD function only gives the part that is left over. In the above example, the function would produce the remainder 1. (@MOD (9,4)

Task — Produce the number 3.14159 (pi)
Function — @PI
Explanation — This simply calls up pi. (The number itself is inserted, instead of the user having to write it out.)

Task — Produce a random number
Function — @RAND
Explanation — Symphony has a *random number generator*. This function produces a positive number *less* than 1. It is useful in applications where a different number is needed each time the formula is run.

Business Functions

Task — Find the *future value* of a stream of payments
Function — @FV
Explanation — The best way to understand future value is to see an example. Let's say that we open a savings account, into which we place $500 each year. If we assume an interest rate of 10 percent compounded annually, and we make our contribution each year, how much money will we have in 12 years?
  The formula to express this is:

@FV(500,10%,12)

which yields, $12,066.56. ($500 at 10 percent, compounded annually over 12 years.)
  Many times you will want the future value based on a monthly calculation rather than an annual calculation. For example, you have a second mortgage on your house. The payments are $100 per month, at 12 percent interest for five years. What is the total amount you will have paid out after three years?
  Here you are concerned with a stream of payments which are compounded monthly. The formula, then, must reflect this:

@FV(100,12%/12,3*12)

which yields $4307.68. This translates as 100 dollars a month, 12 percent interest (divided by 12 so that it will be compounded monthly), and three years (times 12 months, so that we get 36 payments). There are three entries to be made. The first is the amount of the payment (assuming an equal stream of payments). The second is the interest rate charged. The third is the number of payments. The result will be the total value of the annuity (the stream of payments) after the final payment. The formula is expressed in years.

Task — Find the present value of a stream of payments
Function — @PV
Explanation — It is incorrect to say that the present value of an annuity (a stream of payments) is the opposite of the future value, yet it is done frequently. While the calculations are similar, they are used for different purposes. In most instances future value is used to determine how much money, in *nominal* dollars, an annuity will yield over a period of time. Present value, on the other hand, attempts to determine the value of an annuity in terms of *real* dollars. The difference is subtle, yet important.

An example may help to clarify this point. Let's say that someone asks you to lend him $2,000. He agrees to repay the debt in two payments of $1,000 each, over the next two years. What is today's value of that $2,000, which you will not fully receive for two years? Today's value is not $2,000. After all, you could invest that money in a savings account and earn perhaps 10 percent interest compounded on it, over the same two year period. You will lose that interest if you don't invest the money. Hence, today's value of the $2,000 is less. To find out how much less you use the formula:

@PV(1000,.10,2)

which yields $1,735.54. The loss is $264.46.

Knowing this, you can make a loan without losing money. You could loan this person $1,735.54 today if he agreed to repay $2,000. That way, you wouldn't lose any money. (Of course, you wouldn't make much either. You'd probably want to charge a higher rate of interest than a bank would yield because of the added risk.)

There are three entries to be made in this formula. The first is the amount of the payment. The second is the interest rate. The third is the number of payments. The interest rate is compounded annually (unless you divide by 12 for monthly compounding). The entry for the number of payments is assumed to be in years. For months, multiply by 12 (after changing the interest rate compounding).

Task — Find the present value of an uneven stream of payments
Function — @NPV
Explanation — This differs from the present value function just discussed, in that the payments are not equal. There are only two types of entry. After the function symbol, the first entry is the *interest rate*, which is assumed to be constant. The next entry is a *range* of each of the payments.

As an example, assume you are investing in a tax shelter. The shelter first involves making contributions. However, after a period of time, it starts yielding a positive cash flow. You want to find out what the present value is of this uneven series of payments over the five year period you anticipate owning the shelter. Here are the payments:

	A	B
1	YEAR	AMOUNT
2	1	− 2,500 (Minus sign indicates a contribution)
3	2	− 1,000
4	3	500
5	4	1,200
6	5	3,000
7		12%

To find the present value of this stream of funds, you would first enter each of the payments in a cell. Then enter the interest rate in another cell. (The formula would use cell numbers instead of the actual values.) Assuming the interest rate was in cell B7 (12%) and the values were in cells B2. .B6, you would use the following formula:

@NPV(B7,B2. .B6)

which would yield – $208.54.

Task — Find the monthly (annual) payment on a mortgage
Function — @PMT
Explanation — You must know the principal amount, the interest rate and the term. The formula assumes the term will be in years, so you must convert to months. The entry form is principal first, interest second, and term last.

   This formula is a must if you're involved with any type of financing. It is also extremely easy to use. For example, to find the monthly payment on a car loan of $5,000 at 18 percent interest over five years, the following formula can be used:

@PMT(5000,.18/12,5*12)

which yields $126.97 per month. (The principal amount of $5,000, the interest rate divided by 12 so that it will be compounded monthly, and the years multiplied by 12 so the payments will be calculated monthly.)

Task — Find the internal rate of return
Function — @IRR
Explanation — This function requires that you guess at the internal rate of return. Your guess is simply a starting point for Symphony to begin its calculations. You can guess anywhere between 0 and 100 percent (0 and 1). After your guess, type in the cash flow in terms of a range. Symphony will produce an approximate internal rate of return.

   The IRR is used to determine what rate of return is required to justify a series of cash flows. Put another way, it is the return rate required to balance what you put into a project with what you get out of it.

   To illustrate this further, suppose you are purchasing a truck as an investment. The initial cost is $25,000. You will lease it out for four years at $12,000 a year, at which time you will sell it as scrap for $4,000. What is your IRR?

	A
1	– 25,000
2	12,000
3	12,000
4	12,000
5	12,000
6	4,000

The formula would be:

@IRR(.25,A1. .A5)

which would yield 34.65 percent. (The .25 was your guess, the range is the full values during the time of ownership.)

Statistical Functions

Task — Find the minimum value in a range of numbers
Function — @MIN
Explanation — This function searches a range of values and extracts the minimum value. For example, in the series, "4,3,7,5", this function will extract 3. The form is:

@MIN(A1. . .A5)

Task — Find the maximum value in a range of numbers
Function — @MAX
Explanation — This searches a range of values and extracts the maximum value. Applying the function below to the series, "4,3,7,5", would produce 7. The form is:

@MAX(A1. .A5)

Task — Find the average of values in a range
Function — @AVG
Explanation — This searches a range of values and calculates the average value. In the series, "4,3,5,7" the average would be 4.75. The form is:

@AVG(4,3,7,5)

Task — Find the number of occupied cells in a range
Function — @COUNT
Explanation — Symphony counts through a range and displays the number of occupied cells. The form is:

@COUNT(A1. .A9)

Note: if only one cell is counted, the result will be 1, even if the cell is empty.

Task — Find the standard deviation in a range of values
Function — @STD
Explanation — Symphony examines a range of numbers to find the standard deviation. (The standard deviation is used to determine if the values in a range are grouped tightly together near the mean value, or are spread apart.) The form is:

@STD(A1. .A10.)

Task — Find the variance in a range of values
Function — @VAR
Explanation — Symphony examines a range of numbers to find the variance. (The variance is used to determine how far single values differ from the overall group. It is the square root of the standard deviation.) The form is:

@VAR(F5. .F15)

Time and Date Functions

Symphony converts all time and date references to numbers. It begins by arbitrarily assigning the number 1 to the date, January 1, 1900, and adds one number for each date until it arrives at the final date, which is 73050, representing December 31, 2099. Symphony can handle any date occurring during that two century range. (If you want a date outside the range, you're out of luck!)

Time is handled similarly. Each hour, minute and second are given a different decimal number between 0 and 1. One second before midnight, for example, is .9999999. Midnight itself, however, becomes .0.

All of this can be somewhat confusing. Whenever we enter a date or time in a cell in the worksheet, we get one of these imposing numbers. For example, were we to enter three fifteen and 20 seconds, then .135590 would appear in the cell.

While this makes perfect sense to Symphony, it tends to create confusion for most users.

Therefore, entering time and date in Symphony becomes a two-step process. We've just described the first step, entering the time and/or date. The second step is making it comprehensive.

This is actually quite simple. First, call up the MENU and select FORMAT, then DATE or TIME. You are then given the following options:

DATE
1 (DD-MMM-YY) 2(DD-MMM) 3(MMM-YY) 4(Full Intn'l) 5(Partial)

TIME
1(HH:MM:SS AM/PM) 2(HH:MM AM/PM) 3(Full Intn'l) 4(Partial)

Depending on what you select, you can format one or more cells (using the range option) to present date and time as we humans understand it. *Note*: if you select any but the last date or time option, you will get a series of asterisks across the cell indicating that there isn't enough width to display your selection. You can either enlarge the column, or go back and temporarily select option 5.

Using the Date and Time Code

Once you have converted time and dates to Symphony's code, you can then use them in formulas as you would any other values.

Task — Insert a date
Function — @DATE
Explanation — To enter the date, the following format *must* be followed:

Year first (85)
Month second (12)
Day last (31)

A correct entry will look like this:

@DATE(85,12,31)

The entry will be displayed as Symphony's code number 31412, which can then be converted to several date options, using MENU, FORMAT, DATE.

Task — Insert a time
Function — @TIME
Explanation — To enter the time, the following format *must* be followed:

Hour first (based on a 24-hour military clock)
Minute next
Second last

The form is:

@TIME(09,25,15)

The entry will be displayed as Symphony's code number .392534, which can later be converted to several time options using MENU, FORMAT, TIME.

Task — Enter a date, using foreign format
Function — @DATEVALUE
Explanation — Symphony can accept dates from other programs such as dBASE II or III. The format is written as a label into a cell. For example, cell number X1 might contain '1-Jan-84. (Remember, ' is a code prefix, indicating *flush left*. See Chapter 4.) The form for translating this to Symphony's code would be:

@DATEVALUE(X1)

which would yield 30682.

Task — Enter a time using a foreign format
Function — @TIMEVALUE

Explanation — As noted for @DATEVALUE, a foreign format can be translated to Symphony's code. For example, 10:30 am, placed in cell X1 would use the:

@TIMEVALUE(X1)

which would yield .4375

Task — Enter today's date and time
Function — @NOW
Explanation — This function does not require an argument. Simply placing it into a cell will call up the current date and time. *Note*: Symphony doesn't possess a clock or a calendar. It takes the date and time from the Disk Operating System. This means you must enter the correct date and time when you begin working on your computer in order for Symphony to interpret it. The date and time are updated every time the sheet is recalculated.

Task — Find the day only, from a date entry
Function — @DAY
Explanation — Strips and displays the day from a date. If cell X1 contains @DATE(85,12,1), the form is:

@DAY(X1)

which yields 1.

Task — Find the month only, from a date entry
Function — @MONTH
Explanation — This strips and displays the month from a date. If cell X1 contains @DATE(85,12,1), the form is:

@MONTH(X1)

which yields 12.

Task — Find the year only, from a date entry
Function — @YEAR
Explanation — This strips and displays the year from a date. For example, if cell X1 contains @DATE(85,12,1) the form is:

@YEAR(X1)

which yields 85.

Task — Find the second only, from a time entry
Function — @SECOND
Explanation — Strips the second entry from a time entry. If cell X1 contains @TIME(5,25,17), the form is:

@SECOND(X1)

which yields 17.

Task — Find the minute only, from a time entry
Function — @MINUTE
Explanation — Strips the minute entry from a time entry. If cell X1 contains @TIME(5,25,17), the form is:

MINUTE(X1)

which yields 25.

Task — Find the hour only, from a time entry
Function — @TIME
Explanation — Strips the hour entry from a time entry. If cell X1 contains @TIME(5,25,17), the form is:

@HOUR(X1)

which yields 5.

Label (String) Functions

As noted in the last chapter, Symphony contains a number of functions which specifically aid in the handling of *labels* or *strings*. There are two special rules that pertain to these functions. For example, the functions may only allow for string input. If you input a value (number) you may get an ERROR reading. In addition, to allow Symphony to handle strings, the functions assign each character a number, starting from the left most position (after the prefix). The first character after the prefix is 0, the next is 1, the next 2, and so forth.

Task — Change all the characters in a label to upper case
Function — @UPPER
Explanation — The correct form is *either*:

@UPPER(X1) or @UPPER("Peter Piper")

Note: if Peter Piper is written out (literal string), it must be enclosed by quotation marks. If it had been previously written into a cell, just calling up that cell's number will do. The result will be PETER PIPER.

Task — Change all the characters in a label to lower case
Function — @LOWER
Explanation — The correct form is *either*:

@LOWER(X1) or @LOWER("Peter Piper")

Note: if Peter Piper is written out (literal string), it must be enclosed by quotation marks. If it has been previously written into a cell, just calling up that cell's number will do. The result will be, peter piper.

Task — Change a label to initial caps
Function — @PROPER
Explanation — The correct form is *either*:

@PROPER(X1) or @PROPER ("PETER PIPER")

Note: if PETER PIPER is written out (literal string), it must be enclosed by quotation marks. If it has been previously written into a cell, just calling up that cell's number will do. The result will be, Peter Piper.

Task — Find a specified number of characters on the left of a string
Function — @LEFT
Explanation — Allows the user to strip as many characters as desired, starting from the left of a string. If cell X1 contains 'Peter Piper, the first three letters on the left, for example, can be stripped with the form:

@LEFT(X1,3)

which yields, Pet. (Either a cell location or a literal string in quotes will work.)

Task — Find a specified number of characters on the right of a string
Function — @RIGHT
Explanation — Allows the user to strip as many characters as desired, starting from the right of a string. If cell X1 contains 'Peter Piper, the first four letters on the right can be stripped with the form:

@RIGHT(X1,4)

which yields, iper. (Either a cell location or a literal string in quotes will work.)

Task — Find a specified number of characters in the middle of a string.
Function — @MID
Explanation — In order to find characters in the middle, it is first necessary to *identify* the middle. This is done by indicating characters from the left. Excluding the prefix, Symphony counts the first character as zero, the next as 1 and so on. Once the middle is

established, it is then necessary to tell Symphony how many characters to extract *starting at the middle and moving to the right*. For cell X1 containing Peter Piper, to extract ip, the correct form is:

@MID(X1,7,2)

which yields ip. The formula reads: Cell X1, 8 places from the left (remember the first place is 0), 2 characters.

Task — Find the length of a string
Function — @LENGTH
Explanation — Use this to find how many characters there are in a string. The form is:

@LENGTH(X1)

which yields the number of characters in the label in cell X1.

Task — Remove beginning and ending spaces from a string label
Function — @TRIM
Explanation — Use this to clean up a label which has spaces preceding or following it. The form is:

@TRIM(X1)

If the cell X1 has a label in it, the preceding, as well as trailing spaces (if any) will be removed.

Task — Remove control codes from a label
Function — @CLEAN
Explanation — Control codes tell a computer and a printer how to function, and are used frequently in word processing. Some labels will have these codes embedded next to the text, particularly if the string originated in Symphony's word processing. To remove these codes use the form:

@CLEAN(X1)

If cell X1 has any control codes, they will be removed.

Task — Repeat a string within a cell
Function — @REPEAT
Explanation — This repeats the string (label) as many times as desired within the target cell. The form is:

@REPEAT(X1,3)

If the cell X1 contains the label "help", it will be repeated three times in the target cell.

Task — Convert a numeric label to a value
Function — @VALUE
Explanation — Occasionally, you may type in a number, particularly in word processing, that is taken literally as a string. It will usually have the prefix ' before it. This can be converted to a true number with the form:

@VALUE(X1)

If X1 has a string value, '789, it will be converted to the numeric value, 789.

Task — Convert a numeric value into a string
Function — @STRING
Explanation — This is close to the opposite of @VALUE, described above. It converts the value 789, to string '789.

Besides the fact that as a value, 789 is on the right side of the cell, and as a string it is on the left, there is another important difference. As a value, 789 can be used in a formula, as a string it cannot. Yet, even though '789 is a string, *it changes if its underlying cell changes during a calculation.* Thus the string, '789, could be inserted in text, and would still change if its underlying cell also changed. The form is:

@STRING(X1,0)

If the cell X1 contains the value 789, it will be converted to the string, '789 with no decimal places. The last entry (in this case 0) refers to the number of decimal places you want Symphony to enter.

Task — Find a substring within a string
Function — @FIND
Explanation — This is a search function. Symphony will search a string and tell you the location of a specific substring. If, in cell X1, we have Peter Piper and we want to know the location of the substring Piper, we can use the following:

@FIND("Piper",X1,0)

The result will be 6, the location of the start of the substring, Piper. To reach this point you would:

1. Type the function, @FIND
2. Type the substring, Piper
3. Type the cell to search, X1
4. Type the spot to start the search, in this case the far left side, 0.

Task — Replace a substring within a string
Function — @REPLACE
Explanation — This performs the same function as @FIND, only in addition to finding, it also replaces a substring. If in cell X1, we have Peter Piper, and we want to replace Piper with Smith, we can accomplish this with the following:

@REPLACE(X1,6,5,"Smith")

which yields Peter Smith. To do this you would:

1. Type the function, @REPLACE.

2. Type the cell to search, X1.

3. Type the location in the target string where replacement is to begin, 6. (In this case it is 7 characters from the left. Remember, the first character is 0).

4. Type the number of characters to replace, in this case 5.

5. Type in the replacement, in this case, Smith. (Don't forget the quotation marks when typing a literal string.)

Task — Display the first character in a string in ASCII
Function — @CODE
Explanation — ASCII is a standardized code that most computers use to *transmit information*. Each letter or character is represented by a different code number between 0 and 255. To find the number for the first character in a string use the form:

@CODE(X1)

If cell X1 contains the string Peter Piper, the code that is returned will be 80, which is ASCII (decimal) for P.

Task — Display a character when given the ASCII value.
Function — @CHAR
Explanation — Same procedure as above, but gives the character when ASCII code is known.

True/False Functions

These logical functions are primarily of concern to advanced users of Symphony. They always produce one of two answers: 1 = TRUE or 0 = FALSE. We will mention them briefly here:

Task — Ask the question, true or false?
Function — @IF
Form — @IF(NUMBER, T-VALUE, F-VALUE)

Task — Return true (1)
Function — @TRUE

Task — Return false (0)
Function — @FALSE

Task — Find out if ERR is in a cell
Function — @ISERR
Form — @ISERR(X1)

Task — Find out if NA is in a cell
Function — @ISNA
Form — @ISNA(X1)

Task — Find out if a cell contains a string
Function — @ISSTRING
Form — @ISSTRING (X1)

Task — Find out if a cell contains a value
Function — @ISNUMBER
Form — @ISNUMBER (X1)

Look-Up Functions

Finally, Symphony also contains a number of *look-up* functions that can be helpful to advanced users. Again, we'll just briefly mention them here:

Task — Indicate an error
Function — @ERR

Task — Indicate "Not Available" in a cell
Function — @NA

Task — Compare indicator to a value in a table.
Function — @VLOOKUP (COLUMN VALUE)
Function — @HLOOKUP (ROW VALUE)
Form — @VLOOKUP (Select Indicator, Range, Offset)

Task — Select a value within a range
Function — @INDEX
Form — @INDEX (Range, column number, row number)

Task — Pick an argument out
Function — @CHOOSE
Form — @CHOOSE (Criteria value, first argument, more arguments)

Task — Get information about a cell
Function — @CELL
Function — @CELL POINTER (Goes to last cell reference)
Form — @CELL (Identifying value, range)

Task — Find the number of columns or rows in a range
Function — @COLS
Function — @ROWS
Form — @COLS(B2. .H20)

CHAPTER
8

Symphony's
Windows

As we've seen, Symphony opens only one spreadsheet at a time. However, that spreadsheet is enormous, so large that we can only see a tiny fraction of it at any given time on the screen.

We can, move our "window," however so that we can see other portions of the sheet. *Or* we can open other windows and view different parts of the sheet simultaneously. Here's a diagram that shows what we might be able to see with four different windows open (Figure 8.1).

A window, therefore, simply provides a way to see another portion of the sheet. (It's important to understand that a window is *not* an opening to a different sheet.)

Once you grasp the concept of windows, then handling them becomes fairly mechanical. You need to know:

1. How do I open and close windows?

2. How do I manage windows which I've opened?

We'll answer each of these questions in turn, using the **Task/Explanation** format.

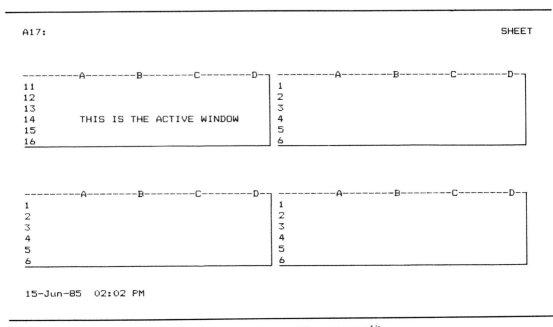

Fig. 8.1 Diagram showing sheet with four different windows on different areas of it.

How to Open and Close Windows

We will consider several ways to accomplish this.

Task — Open a window by splitting the current screen
Command — SERVICES, WINDOW, PANE
Explanation — You can split the current window in half (either vertically or horizontally), or into quarters, with this simple command. Try it and you'll see the results immediately. Each window, however, will be displaying the same thing. To access different data in different windows, you must go to each window and move it to that part of the sheet on which you want to focus. Use the SERVICES Screen, WINDOW, DELETE command to remove unwanted windows. Use the SERVICES Screen, WINDOW, LAYOUT command to increase the size of a window. Figures 8.2 and 8.2A give examples of these splits.

Task — Create a new window
Command — SERVICES, WINDOW, CREATE
Explanation — There are several steps involved in creating a new window. They are all relatively easy to use. The first step is to get to the SERVICES, WINDOW, CREATE MENU. As soon as you do this you are asked:

New Window Name:
MAIN

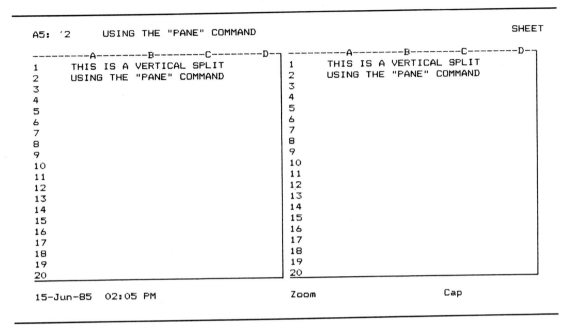

Fig. 8.2 Vertical split using PANE.

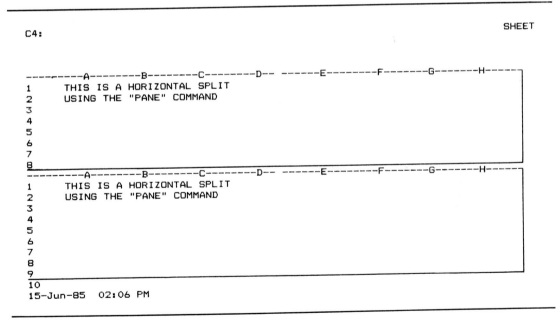

Fig. 8.2A Horizontal split using PANE.

Assuming you only have the window that Symphony opened for you when you started the program, you can now open a second window. (If you have other windows open, they will be listed.) The open window is called MAIN, by default. In order to open a second window, you must now give it a name. Any name of 15 characters or less will do. Try to use something descriptive. In this particular case call the second window, HARRY. As you type it in, it will appear on the upper left of your screen.

As soon as you've given your window a name, you will be asked for its type. You may specify any of the environments that Symphony offers. The most common window types are either document or spreadsheet. (We'll discuss graph windows in a later chapter.) Whatever you specify here will be the opening environment in your window. (Of course, once open, you can change it to a different environment.)

After you've selected your environment, you will be asked to define its layout on the screen, and then to restrict it. These two procedures will be covered in a moment. You can simply hit [**ENTER**] to get past these commands now, and return to them later after you've finished this chapter. Now, by exiting the various menus, you can return to your screen where your new window will have taken shape.

Task — Define the layout of a window
Command — SERVICES, WINDOW, LAYOUT (Also reached automatically when creating a window.)
Explanation — This command asks you to define the part of the screen that your window will occupy. (If you don't specify a part of the screen, the new window will occupy the entire screen.) Use the arrow keys to give your answer.

Using the arrow keys can be tricky, however, because they are anchored. The default finds the screen anchored by its upper left hand corner. (If you can't visualize *anchored*, try the LAYOUT command just described, and use the arrow keys to move the *highlighted* area. You'll find that the arrow keys will move the window up from the bottom, or away from the right side. But they will not move it down from the top, or away from the left side. The window is anchored at the upper left corner.) You can see what I mean in Figure 8.3.

Of course, it's easy enough to change the anchor position because it's controlled by the period key ([.]). Typing the [.] moves the cursor which determines the anchor position. (The cursor is a small dash, barely visible on your screen.) The default cursor position is the lower right hand corner. Typing the [.] once, moves the cursor to the lower left hand side of the window. Now you can move the highlighted area up or to the right, but not to the left. (It's anchored in the upper right hand corner.) Thereafter, each time you type [.], the cursor moves around the window clockwise to the next corner. The anchor is diagonally across the screen from the cursor. Figure 8.4 shows the period positions around the window.

By changing the location of the anchor, you can create a window on *any* part of your screen. Once the window is created, you can move it to another part of the screen using the [**SCROLL-LOCK**].

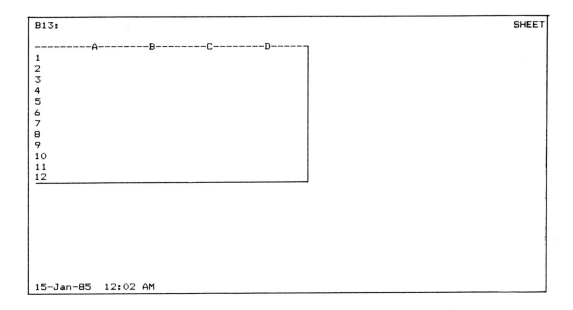

Fig. 8.3 Diagram showing window moved part way in from bottom and left.

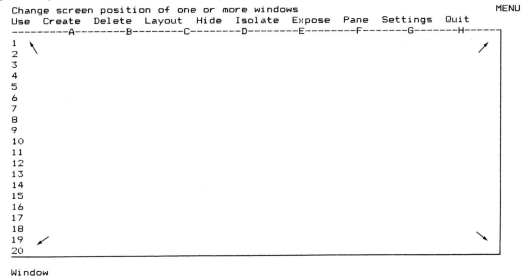

Fig. 8.4 Diagram of period positions around the window.

Task — Move a partial window to a different spot on the screen
Command — SERVICES, WINDOW, LAYOUT, SCROLL-LOCK KEY
Explanation — Once you have created a window and laid it out on the screen, you may find you want it to be in a different position. You can move the window you have

created **anywhere** on the screen (even over the top of other windows) by using [**SCROLL-LOCK**] while you are in the LAYOUT command. [**SCROLL-LOCK**] gives your arrow keys new capability, allowing them to move the created partial window anywhere you want on the screen.

Task — Delete a window
Command — SERVICES, WINDOW, DELETE KEY
Explanation — You can easily delete any window in the worksheet (except the last window; Symphony demands that at least one window be open at all times) with this command. It will show you a directory. Then you use the arrow keys to indicate which window is to be removed. *Note*: you can *only* remove one window at a time. Symphony has no facility for removing many windows simultaneously.

How to Manage a Window

Managing windows includes both the movement of windows to different parts of the sheet, as well as the handling of many windows simultaneously.

Task — Move a window around the sheet
Command — DIRECTIONAL KEYS OR GOTO KEY ([**F5**])
Explanation — You move a window around the spreadsheet by moving the cursor or the pointer within it. For example, let's say you are in the MAIN window, which Symphony opens for you. You are viewing columns A-H and rows 1-20. You now want to see column J. Simply move your pointer to the far right of your screen, until you reach the end. Continue moving it. Your window will automatically scroll to the right, exposing more of the worksheet until you can see column J. Similarly, if you want to see other rows, move your pointer down (in this case), until it goes to the bottom of the window. When you reach row 20, your pointer will drag the window down, exposing more of the sheet below. Figure 8.5 shows you what I mean.

Essentially the same rules apply for moving additional windows as apply for moving the original window. If you hit [**CONTROL + RIGHT ARROW**] when you are in the sheet environment, you will be moved approximately one window at a time to the right. [**CONTROL + LEFT ARROW**]moves you one window to the left. [**PAGE UP**] and [**PAGE DOWN**] move you a window up or down. Using [**END**] together with arrow keys takes you either to the end of the sheet, or to the next group of cells in the direction that you are going.

In addition, you can use the GOTO key to transport your window immediately to any other position on the sheet. *Note*: two windows can view the same or different parts of the sheet.

Task — Restrict the range of a window
Command — SERVICES, WINDOW, SETTINGS, RESTRICT
Explanation — You can *restrict* a window so that it only views one portion of a sheet.

Moving window around sheet.

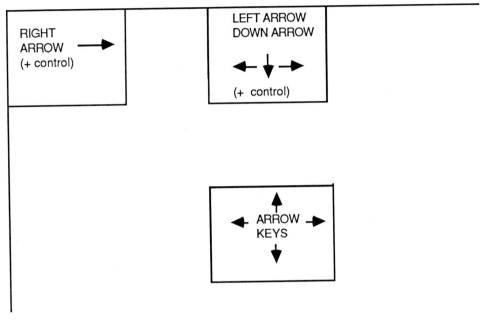

Fig. 8.5 Moving a Window.

In this case, Symphony will "beep" when you try to go beyond the restricted limits, and you will not be able to move the pointer out of the restricted area.

When you issue the RESTRICT command you will be offered three options:

SCREEN, RANGE, NONE

The first option, SCREEN, will restrict the pointer to the area just shown on your screen. You will not be able to go beyond the bounds of what you see.

The second option, RANGE, allows you to enter a range that you want restricted. You select the boundaries. (See Chapter 5 on ranges.)

The last option, NONE, indicates that the window will be completely unrestricted, as before. Figure 8.6 illustrates the RESTRICT RANGE MENU.

Task — Change windows
Command — WINDOW KEY
Command — SERVICES, WINDOW, USE
Explanation — Although there is technically no limit to the number of windows you can have, there can only be *one* active window at a time, regardless of how many windows you may have open. You can use this command to determine which window

```
Restrict pointer movement to range currently on screen          MENU
Screen   Range   None
┌────────────────────────────────────────────────────────────────┐
│   Name:        MAIN                                             │
│   Type:        SHEET                                            │
│   Restrict:    A1..IV8192                                       │
│   Borders:     None                                            │
│   Auto-Display: Yes                                            │
└──────────────────────────────────────────Window Settings──────┘
```

Fig. 8.6 RESTRICT RANGE MENU.

will be active. To *thumb through* the windows that are open, making each one active in turn, use the WINDOW key ([**F6**]). Each time you tap it you'll be moved to a new window (Figure 8.7).

To move to a specific window, try the USE command. When you get to USE, the screen will display a directory of all the windows you have created. (Hit MENU to see other windows, if there isn't enough room on the command line to display all of them.) Use the arrow keys to indicate which window you want to be active. As soon as you enter this information (carriage return), the appropriate window will become active, as indicated by the cursor or pointer in that window.

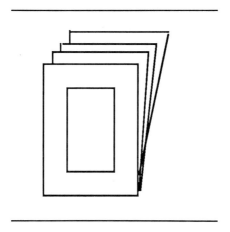

Fig. 8.7 Illustration of thumbing through windows.

Partial Windows

Task — Locate covered windows

Command — SERVICES, WINDOW, USE

Explanation — Sometimes you have both full screen windows and smaller partial windows. When the full screen window is active, it will totally cover the partial window (or any other full screen window). You will think that the covered windows have been lost.

They aren't. They are merely covered. The USE command will call up the directory of all the windows. Specify which one you want to be active and it will immediately appear.

Task — Isolate a window
Command — SERVICES, WINDOW, ISOLATE
Explanation — Sometimes it is distracting to have more than one window on a screen. For example, you may have two windows showing, one full screen, the other partial. When the partial window is active, it is superimposed on the full screen window as illustrated in Figure 8.8 below.

```
B2:  'PAYMENTS                                                                SHEET

----------A---------B---------C--------D--------E--------F--------G-------H-----┐
1              INVENTORY OF AVAILABLE PRODUCTS
2              HAMMERS  DRIVERS  PULLERS  TROWELLS BENCHES
3                  4        34       3       1        0
4                  3         5       3       0        0
5                  6         6       3       0        0
6                  4         7    ----------A--------B--------C--------D--------E┐┐
7                  7        65    1      PAYMENTS                                │
8                  3         3    2      Caprolls Treetops Shoehorns            │
9                  1        56    3        $234      $45      $43               │
10                65         9    4        $34       $67      $453              │
11                 9        45    5        $567      $44      $323              │
12                65         3    6        $224      $33      $7,789            │
13                 3         5    7        $67       $99      $53               │
14                 6         8    8        $789      $65      $55               │
15                 7         6    9        $234      $23      $22               │
16                 3         4    10       $579      $998     $789              │
17                 2        65    11       $89       $334     $2,332            │
18                 5        45    12       $234      $6       $44               │
19                 6         2    13       $2,234    $331     $678              │
20                 3         4    14       $2,152    $665     $43               │
                   4        78    15       $5,434    $989     $34               │
15-Jan-85   12:25 AM
```

Fig. 8.8 Diagram of partial window on top of full window.

You may want to see *only* the partial window, yet not delete the full window. Use the ISOLATE command. *All* windows other than the current window will disappear from the screen (Figure 8.9).

You can restore all the windows to the screen by using the EXPOSE command, or restore only one window by using the WINDOW, USE command.

Task — Hide a window
Command — SERVICES, WINDOW, HIDE
Explanation — You may have a whole series of windows that are open, and you are thumbing through them using the WINDOW key ([**F6**]). You find, however, that you are really only using two or three of the whole stack. Yet, when you use [**F6**], you must thumb through all of them.

```
Make a window current                                            MENU
Use   Create   Delete   Layout   Hide   Isolate   Expose   Pane   Settings   Quit



                    ---------A---------B---------C---------D---------E---¬
                    1              PAYMENTS
                    2              Caprolls Treetops Shoehorns
                    3                 $234      $45       $43
                    4                  $34      $67      $453
                    5                 $567      $44      $323
                    6                 $224      $33    $7,789
                    7                  $67      $99       $53
                    8                 $789      $65       $55
                    9                 $234      $23       $22
                    10                $579     $998      $789
                    11                 $89     $334    $2,332
                    12                $234       $6       $44
                    13              $2,234     $331      $678
                    14              $2,152     $665       $43
                    15              $5,434     $989       $34
Window
```

Fig. 8.9 Diagram of isolating a window.

You can use the HIDE command to remove the list of windows that can be activated using [F6]. Thus, you can then easily toggle back and forth between the several windows you are currently working with. EXPOSE returns all windows to the list of those which can be activated, as does USE.

Task — Expose all windows
Command — SERVICES, WINDOW, EXPOSE
Explanation — Allows all windows to become current in turn.

Task — Explode the size of a partial window
Command — ZOOM KEY
Explanation — Sometimes you may momentarily want to "explode" the size of a window that's smaller than our screen. Rather than going to the trouble of changing the layout twice (once to make it larger, once again to make it smaller), you can use the ZOOM key ([ALT] plus [F6]).

Hitting ([ALT] plus [F6]) explodes the window to the full size of the screen. Hitting them again cuts its back to its former size.

Task — Remove the borders of a window
Command — SERVICES, WINDOW, SETTINGS, BORDER
Explanation — Sometimes you might want to simply display the contents of a document or sheet without the format display (letters and numbers on a sheet) appearing. The above command can be used to accomplish this. You are then given three

options: the first displays the window you usually see; the second shows borders with lines only; and the third shows no borders at all.

Task — Switch between different types of windows
Command — SWITCH KEY ([**ALT**] plus [**F9**])
Explanation — Once you have established a window, Symphony provides a quick and simple way of switching back and forth between environments. For example, you may want your window to switch rapidly from being a document window to a sheet window, and back again.

Using the above command, Symphony quickly switches you back and forth between the current window type and the *last window type selected.*

For example, the default is a sheet window. Now, let's say you create a DOC window. However, you want to see something you've written in a SHEET environment. Hitting SWITCH ([**ALT**] plus [**F9**] instantly switches you back to SHEET. Hit the keys again and you are instantly back in the DOC environment.

Suppose, however, that you are in DOC and you want to go to a graph. You must call up the TYPE MENU ([**ALT**] plus [**F10**]) and select GRAPH. When you are there, you decide you want to go back to a document. Since DOC was the last environment you used before changing to GRAPH, simply use SWITCH ([**ALT**] plus [**F9**]), and you'll instantly be there. In this manner you can toggle back and forth between documents and graphs.

Remember, the toggle only works between the current and the last environment used. It will not automatically take you back to the SHEET environment.

≡Summary

We've looked at ways to *window* in Symphony. While at first these processes may seem strange, what should become clear to you is that using windows is extremely easy.

Document and sheet windows will operate almost identically as described in this chapter. Graph windows require some special understanding, which will be covered in the specific section on graphs. Form and Communications windows are also different, and will be covered in detail in special sections further on in this book, as well.

CHAPTER
9

Creating Your
First Graph

One of the biggest plusses Symphony offers is a quick and easy method of creating graphs on your screen. It offers a highly sophisticated means of printing out graphs, as well.

Constructing basic graphs is extremely easy; in fact with Symphony, the process is virtually foolproof. On the other hand, Symphony enables you to make the graphs as complex as you want.

In this chapter we'll draw our first graph. Then in the proceeding chapters we'll go on to more sophisticated graphs.

The types of graphs that Symphony offers include:

bar (and stacked bar)
XY
pie
line
high-low

The beauty of Symphony's graph system is that once you've established the parameters for one kind of graph, you can instantly switch to another. For example, you might begin with a bar graph. Having once set it up, you might then wonder what the same information would look like on a pie graph. It's only a few keys away.

⫴nformation for Graphs

The basis of the graphics environment is the spreadsheet. The data that the various graphs visually portray comes from the spreadsheet. Thus to create a graph, all that you need to do is specify a particular portion of a spreadsheet that you want to see rendered in graphic form. It's presented almost immediately. The best way of understanding this is to look at a specific example.

Creating a Simple Bar Graph

You can use data from an existing spreadsheet, or you can work with the data presented here. I am going to assume you are starting with a new spreadsheet; and that you'll start at A1. However, you can just as easily use an existing sheet and simply designate ranges for the graph.

Start with the Spreadsheet

Remember, the graph is based on the spreadsheet. That is why you want to start there. It won't do to simply call up GRAPH from the ENVIRONMENT MENU. All we'll get is an empty screen. (However, later on, when you get more proficient at creating graphs, calling up GRAPH in this fashion can actually save time.)

For now let's assume that you have a spreadsheet that looks like this:

```
    ----A---------B---------C--------D---------E-------F--------G--------H---
    1Calif.  Nev.      Ari.      N.Y.     Miss.    Fla.     Tex.     Ill.
    1    230        578       12        867      132      431      502      447
```

Fig. 9.1 Spreadsheet that shows numbers labels.

This is a listing of sales in different states. You want to develop a graph that shows how these sales stack up against each other. To create a bar graph of these figures *when you are in a spreadsheet environment*, you call up:

MAIN
GRAPH

This takes you to the GRAPH MENU. The GRAPH MENU looks like this:

PREVIEW   1st SETTINGS   2nd SETTINGS   IMAGE-SAVE   QUIT

Here's what the various settings mean:

PREVIEW — this allows you to see the graph on the screen, (to preview it before you print it out.)

1st SETTINGS/2nd SETTINGS — These designate the places where you will *set up* what is going into the graph. There are too many settings for one menu line, hence there are two menu lines. You can easily switch back and forth between them.

IMAGE-SAVE — This saves a graph that you want to print out. *Note: you must use* IMAGE-SAVE *if you want to print out. Simply using* SAVE *from the* SERVICES MENU (FILE) *will not allow you to print the graph.*

Since you're creating a graph, begin by taking the 1st SETTINGS choice.
Instantly, your sheet vanishes and you see the first half of the settings sheet, which looks like Figure 9.2.

```
Switch to 2nd-Settings                                              MENU
Switch   Type   Range   Hue   Format   Data-Labels   Legend   Cancel   Name   Quit

      Type:        Line

   Range                Hue   Format   Data-Labels          Legend

   X                    1
   A                    2    Both
   B                    3    Both
   C                    4    Both
   D                    5    Both
   E                    6    Both
   F                    7    Both
                                                    Graph 1st-Settings: MAIN
```

Fig. 9.2 Settings Sheet from Graph Menu.

Don't panic if this looks complicated. It's not, and you'll see how it works as we move along. Begin with the first entry, TYPE. When you select this you are asked which one of the six types of graphs you want to create. Let's start with BAR.
The next entry is RANGE. Selecting that, you are next asked to choose the data values on a scale that looks like Figure 9.3.

```
Location of X data values                                          MENU
X   A   B   C   D   E   F   Quit
```

Fig. 9.3 Data Value Scale.

The default is set to X. This represents the values along the bottom of the graph. Typically it is filled with labels. (To fill it in, select X. You are returned immediately to your sheet, where you are asked for the names of the values to put along the bottom of the chart. Respond by using your pointer to highlight the labels (the row with the state names — A1-H1).

As soon as you enter the X range, you are returned to the RANGE MENU. You've labelled the bottom of the graph, but you haven't given it values yet. You must do that at this point. You'll notice that there are seven value range settings (A-F) offered. Select the first, A. Again, you are returned to your chart. Now use the pointer to highlight the numbers that you want to represent graphically (A2. .H2).

When you enter this data you have completed the basic information that is necessary to create a graph. Now you need to view it.

Previewing the Graph

Exit the various menus until you return to the MAIN GRAPH MENU. Then press PREVIEW and your graph immediately appears on the screen. It should look like Figure 9.4.

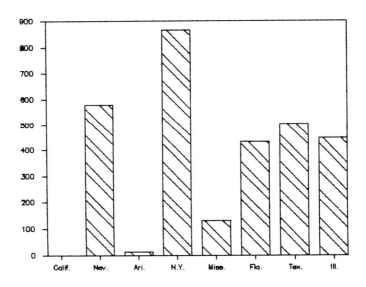

Fig. 9.4 Bar Graph.

If this is your first graph produced on Symphony, you should feel very pleased. However, there is more to come. The way to exit from PREVIEW is by hitting **[ESC]**. Now, let's say that you want to see the information in the form of a line graph. Select 1st SETTINGS, then TYPE, and then LINE. By going back to PREVIEW you can now view the information in the form of a LINE graph, such as appears in Figure 9.5.

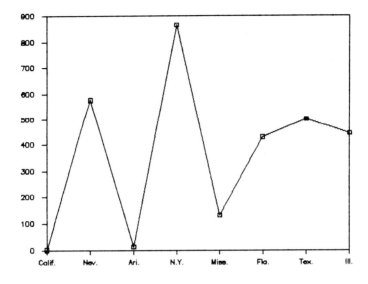

Fig. 9.5 Line Graph.

Returning to TYPE, you can now view it as a pie chart. In fact, you can select any of the choices under TYPE and the appropriate graph form will be displayed. *Note*: some of the choices such as XY or STACKED BAR are not appropriate to the data just entered for this particular graph. Later on we'll see how these are used.

At this point, if you like what you've done, you can now save the graph. To do this, use the IMAGE-SAVE option from the GRAPH MENU, *not the save option from the FILE MENU*. This is because only graphs saved under IMAGE-SAVE can be printed out.

Naming the Graph to be Saved

When you select the IMAGE-SAVE option you are asked what file name to use. Virtually any name will do. However, *do not use a suffix*. (GRAPHA.PIC = Wrong; GRAPHA = Right). Symphony *automatically* adds the suffix .PIC in a format that the printer can later use to print out.

Summary

You should now be able to quickly and easily set up a basic graph. Of course, as with the rest of Symphony, we have only scratched the surface. There are many more sophisticated techniques you can use. We'll examine these, along with printing and *windowing graphs*, in the next chapter.

CHAPTER 10

Enhancing and Printing a Graph

You are now ready to learn how to make more elaborate graphs, how to put different graphs in various windows and attach them to parts of the spreadsheet, and, finally, how to print out. The material is organized in terms of the task to be performed, and the method used to accomplish it. It is assumed that you now have a basic understanding of how to create graphs on Symphony. If you're still unsure of the procedures, then reread the previous chapter.

Enhancing a Graph

In the last chapter we saw how to create a graph when we were in a SPREADSHEET environment. It is also possible to create a graph from a GRAPH environment.

Just call up GRAPH. Your screen will now be blank. To create your graph hit the MENU key ([F10]). Now you'll find the same commands as you reached through the MENU, GRAPH commands of the SHEET environment. Proceed as you did in the last chapter.

The major difference is that with a GRAPH environment, the graph is automatically on your screen and you do not need to use the PREVIEW command. However, you cannot get direct access to the sheet to change values.

Remember, to get to the GRAPH MENU from the GRAPH environment, just hit ([**F10**]). All commands in this chapter will be given for both SHEET and GRAPH environments.

Task — Switch from one type of graph to another
Command — SHEET, MENU, GRAPH, 1st SETTING, TYPE
Command — GRAPH, MENU, 1st SETTING, TYPE
Explanation — From the SHEET environment, use the MENU, GRAPH, 1st SETTINGS, TYPE commands, then select the type of graph you want. From the GRAPH environment, just use the MENU, 1st SETTING, TYPE commands. *Note*: in the GRAPH environment you do not need to use PREVIEW, since as soon as you hit [**ESC**] the graph is automatically on the screen.

Task — Switch from 1st setting to 2nd setting and back
Command — SWITCH
Explanation — When in either setting, the first option on the menu is SWITCH. Use this to switch back and forth between 1st and 2nd SETTINGS.

Working With Bar and Line Graphs

It is important to keep in mind that the X axis is at the *bottom* of a graph. The Y axis is at the *side*. Figure 10.1 clarifies these positions.

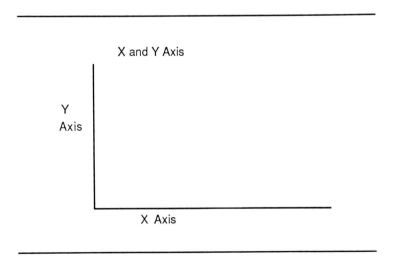

Fig. 10.1 Diagram showing positions of X and Y Axis.

Task — Place labels on the X axis
Command — SHEET, GRAPH, 1st SETTINGS, RANGE
Command — GRAPH, 1st SETTING, RANGE
Explanation — Select the X range. Then use the pointer to indicate the labels or values to be used from the spreadsheet. If you are creating a graph without a spreadsheet, first write the labels into cells, then use this command to insert them into the graph.

Task — Indicate one or more ranges of data to be graphed
Command — SHEET, GRAPH, 1st SETTING, RANGE
Command — GRAPH, 1st SETTING, RANGE
Explanation — Symphony allows up to seven ranges of data to be incorporated into a graph simultaneously. For example, consider the following sheet (Figure 10.2).

Person	1st	2nd	3rd	4th	Totals
Peter	$11,000	$10,000	$7,000	$13,000	$41,000
Sally	$2,500	$4,500	$6,000	$12,000	$25,000
Fred	$4,500	$4,500	$3,700	$4,700	$17,400
Jim	$9,800	$9,500	$15,500	$3,900	$38,700
Lois	$21,000	$13,000	$7,000	$14,000	$55,000
Totals	$48,800	$41,500	$39,200	$47,600	

Fig. 10.2 Sheet showing sales performances of five sales people.

Suppose you want to display the quarterly totals only in a single range. When the various ranges are displayed, select A. As soon as Symphony switches back to the spreadsheet, highlight row 7. This will enter the totals range. Now PREVIEW, or hit [ESC] to return to the graph window to be sure it contains the correct information. The *single* range will look like Figure 10.3.

To display each salesperson's performance, when the ranges are displayed, select a different range for each salesperson. For example, the A range might be for John. Highlight and enter John's data from the sheet on A. The B range might be for Susan. Highlight and enter her data from the sheet on B. When all five salespeople have had their data entered, you will see a *multiple* range like the one in Figure 10.4.

Task — Add titles to the graph
Command — SHEET, GRAPH, 2nd SETTINGS, TITLES
Command — GRAPH, 2nd SETTINGS, TITLES
Explanation — You may add one title and one subtitle to the top of the graph, as well as a separate title for the X and the Y axis. Get to titles through GRAPH, 2nd SETTINGS. Make the appropriate selection and write in your title.

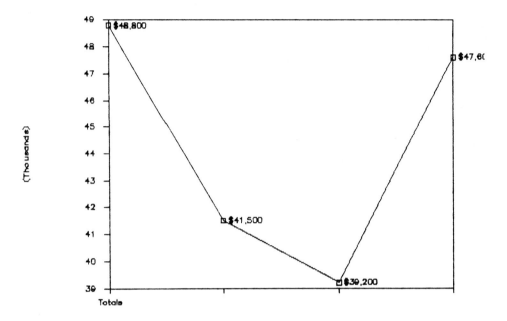

Fig. 10.3 Illustration with One Range.

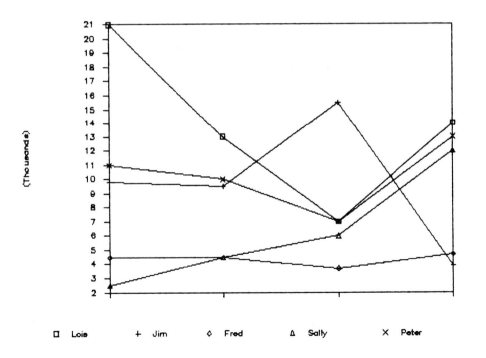

Fig. 10.4 Illustration with Multiple Ranges.

Task — Place floating labels in graph
Command — SHEET, GRAPH, 1st SETTING, DATA-LABEL
Command — GRAPH, 1st SETTING, DATA-LABEL
Explanation — A floating label is identified on a graph by a point, such as the marks illustrated in Figure 10.5.

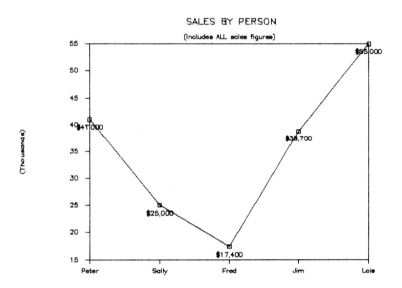

Fig. 10.5 Illustration with Floating Labels.

Floating labels can be created quite easily. You can select which range (A-F) to which you want to supply data-labels. The sheet will now appear and Symphony will ask you to identify the labels to use. The easiest choice is the same data that went into making the range. If that is your selection, then the graph will not only display the graphic representation, but will also indicate the data values for each location on the graph.

You may also select the placement of the label: CENTER, LEFT, ABOVE, RIGHT, BELOW. Experimentation is the best way to find a label location to suit you.

Task — On a line graph, change the display
Command — SHEET, MENU, GRAPH, 1st SETTINGS, FORMAT
Command — GRAPH, MENU, 1st SETTINGS, FORMAT
Explanation — In a graph, the points are displayed as *symbols* and are connected by *lines*. You can choose to have one of the following four selections:

Lines only
Symbols only
Both
Neither

The following two graphs show the differences:

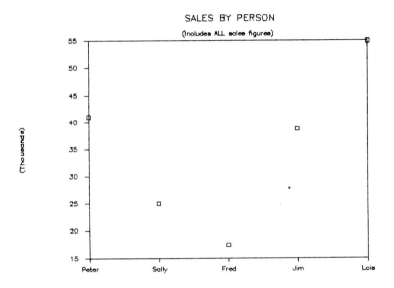

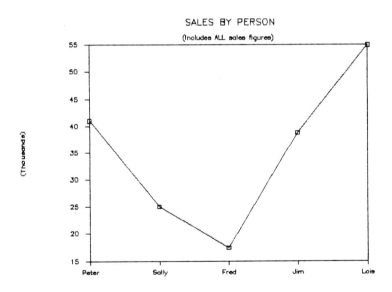

Fig. 10.6, 10.7 Two graphs showing symbols only and lines with symbols.

You can select the display of your choice by choosing GRAPH, FORMAT. *Note*: each line in a line display has different symbols, so that you can tell them apart.

Task — Create a legend for values graphed
Command — SHEET, MENU, GRAPH, 1st SETTINGS, LEGEND

Command — GRAPH, MENU, 1st SETTINGS, LEGEND
Explanation — In a line graph where there are several lines displayed, it is sometimes difficult to discern exactly what the lines refer to. The solution is to have a *legend*. (Remember, each line will have a different symbol for locations on it.) Symphony allows you to create a legend for each line graphed. The legend will appear at the bottom of the graph. It is possible to add a legend for each value range that is plotted.

Note: if you have a color monitor, each line on a line graph, or bar on a bar graph, will appear in a different color. However, when you print out, unless you have a color printer the print-out will be in black and white. In Figure 10.8 you can see a sample of a graph with a legend.

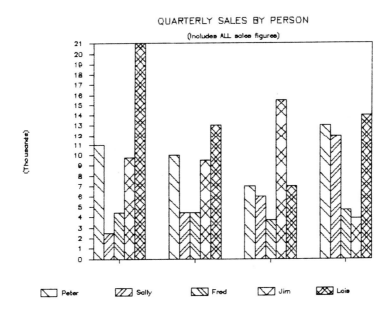

Fig. 10.8 Diagram of Graph with Legends.

Task — Add a grid to a bar graph
Command — SHEET, MENU, GRAPH, 2nd SETTINGS, OTHER, GRID
Command — GRAPH, MENU, 2nd SETTINGS, OTHER, GRID
Explanation — Sometimes, particularly when you are dealing with precise items, it is helpful if you can superimpose a grid over your graph. Then it will look as if you had actually drawn on graph paper.

Symphony offers a grid option. It is attainable through the MENU, GRAPH, 2nd SETTINGS, GRID commands. You are offered the options of vertical grid lines, horizontal grid lines, or a combination of both.

Task — Hide all the text on a graph so only the lines, bars, etc., show
Command — SHEET, MENU, GRAPH, 2nd SETTING, OTHER, HIDE

Command — GRAPH, MENU, 2nd SETTINGS, OTHER, HIDE
Explanation — Sometimes, particularly when you are super-imposing a graph onto a sheet, and are working in a small window, it's difficult to read the legends and labels. If this is the case, Symphony may automatically remove them. However, to see the graph better, we can remove them using the above command.

Task — Add color to a graph
Command — SHEET, MENU, GRAPH, 2nd SETTING, OTHER, COLOR
Command — GRAPH, MENU, 2nd SETTINGS, OTHER, COLOR
Explanation — This is the *color on* or *color off* option. Of course, color will only work if you have a color graphics board and a color monitor attached to your computer, *and* if you have selected a color driver during the INSTALL program.

Task — Change the colors in a graph
Command — SHEET, MENU, GRAPH, 1st SETTING, HUE
Command — GRAPH, MENU, 1st SETTING, HUE
Explanation — The colors in a graph can be controlled through the HUE control found after the MENU, GRAPH, 1st SETTING commands. However, the colors will depend on your hardware. (You can select the colors for all ranges, including the X range.)

Task — Make room in the graph
Command — SHEET, GRAPH, 2nd SETTING, Y-SCALE, WIDTH
Command — SHEET, GRAPH, 2nd SETTING, OTHER, SKIP
Command — GRAPH, 2nd SETTING, Y-SCALE, WIDTH
Command — GRAPH, 2nd SETTING, OTHER, SKIP
Explanation — Occasionally, as you add information to your graph, it can become very cluttered, particularly if you are adding labels and legends. There are two ways of creating more room to work.

The first is to change the width between entries on the Y-scale. Here the default is 9. Simply increase the width to accommodate your needs.

A second, and more effective way to reduce the clutter, is to use the SKIP command. It instructs Symphony to *skip* every other label on the X axis. Since we can usually derive missing labels from those remaining, this can be very helpful.

Task — Raise or lower the bottom of a bar graph
Command — SHEET, MENU, GRAPH, 2nd SETTING, OTHER, ORIGIN
Command — GRAPH, MENU, 2nd SETTING, OTHER ORIGIN
Explanation — Normally, the bars will begin at the bottom of the graph, but you may want them to begin in the middle, or at some other point. (This is particularly useful when describing a minus value.) The origin or starting point of the bars can be manipulated directly using the MENU, GRAPH, 2nd SETTING, OTHER, ORIGIN command. Experiment a bit and you will soon start to pick up very quickly. Simply specify a different origin than the default. Here is an example of a bar graph created by changing the origin.

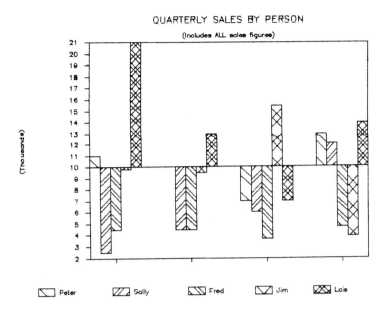

Fig. 10.9 Bar Graph showing below and above the line bars.

Task — Create multiple bars in a graph
Command — SHEET, MENU, GRAPH, 1st SETTINGS, TYPE, BAR
Command — GRAPH, MENU, 1st SETTINGS, TYPE, BAR
Explanation — When you use several ranges (A-F) in a line graph, they appear as different lines on the graph. When you use several ranges in a bar graph, they appear as multiple bars. If you have any problems, create your graph first as a line graph, then switch the TYPE to a bar graph.

Task — Create a stacked bar graph
Command — SHEET, MENU, GRAPH, 1st SETTING, TYPE, STACKED BAR
Command — GRAPH, MENU, 1st SETTING, TYPE, STACKED BAR
Explanation — A stacked bar graph is one in which different ranges are stacked one on top of the other. You can see this in Figure 10.10.

It is essentially the same as a line or a bar graph that has several ranges. The difference is that the ranges are stacked one on top of the other. If you have difficulty working with this type of graph, first create either a line or bar graph with ranges, then simply convert it to a stacked bar graph using the commands shown above.

Working With an X and Y Graph

Task — Create an XY graph
Command — SHEET, MENU, GRAPH, 1st SETTING, TYPE, XY
Command — GRAPH, MENU, 1st SETTING, TYPE, XY

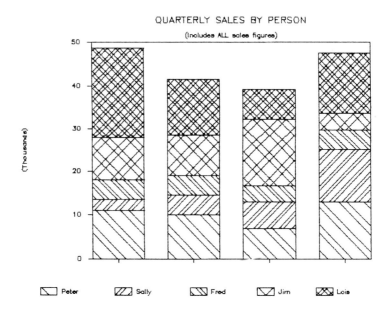

Fig. 10.10 Stacked Bar Graph.

Explanation — An XY graph uses only two ranges, X and Y. In addition, the X range connotes values, instead of labels. Thus, an XY graph plots the relationship of *two sets of values*, X and Y.

After selecting the XY type, enter the *values* in the X and Y range. As soon as you have done this, you can PREVIEW the graph. Sometimes it is helpful to eliminate the lines in an XY graph, and simply use the locations. Use 1st SETTING,FORMAT to depict symbols only. (See Figure 10.11.)

Task — Change the proportions of the X or Y scale
Command — SHEET, MENU, GRAPH, 2nd SETTING, X (or Y) SCALE
Command — GRAPH, MENU, 2nd SETTINGS, X (OR Y) SCALE
Explanation — Symphony automatically formats both the X and Y scale for you when you input the range data. This includes the scale of values and the width of the columns. You can manually override the default settings, however.

When either the X-SCALE or the Y-SCALE are invoked, you are given four options: TYPE, FORMAT, EXPONENT and WIDTH (on the Y scale only). We'll consider each separately.

TYPE refers to the upper and lower value limits of the scale. Invoking this command offers either *automatic, manual* or logarithmic. Under automatic, Symphony sets the limits according to the upper and lower limits of the range you have entered. Under manual, you can set these limits anyplace you choose. Under logarithmic, each new value increases logarithmically over the one before. If you find this difficult to visu-alize, set a simple graph in each of the settings and look at the result.

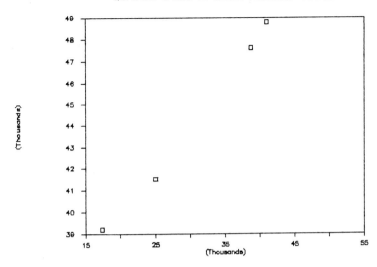

Fig. 10.11 Symbols only on an XY Graph.

FORMAT gives you the same options we found in the SHEET MENU FORMAT, and includes percentages and currency.

EXPONENT refers to the magnitude of numbers displayed. For example, instead of showing the number 50,000, the display might read 50 with a legend that said, (thousands).

Working With a Pie Graph

Task — Create a pie graph
Command — SHEET, MENU, GRAPH, 1st SETTING, TYPE
Command — GRAPH, MENU, 1st SETTING, TYPE
Explanation — You can convert a graph to a pie graph by invoking the PIE selection. The range will be shown as percentages. *Note*: you can select any range from A-F, but only one range can be shown at at time. Figure 10.12 displays a pie graph.

Task — Add labels to a pie graph
Command — SHEET, MENU, GRAPH, 1st SETTING, RANGE
Command — GRAPH, MENU, 1st SETTING, RANGE
Explanation — When you get to the RANGE command, use the X scale to indicate a range of labels. These will then be affixed to the appropriate slices of the pie.

Task — Shade a slice of the pie graph
Command — SHEET, MENU, GRAPH, 1st SETTING, RANGE
Command — GRAPH, MENU, 1st SETTING, RANGE

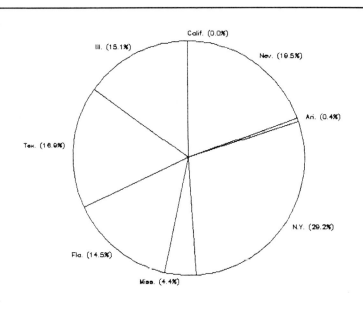

Fig. 10.12 Pie Graph.

Explanation — You can shade individual slices of the pie, either in color or in black and white, depending on your hardware. It's simple to do, but you *must* remember that *the pie graph can only display one range at a time.*

This means that the other ranges are empty. (When we give a range in A, the remaining ranges B-F are unused.) The second range, B, therefore, is used for designating a slice of the pie to be either colored or shaded.

Call up the range setting, and then in the B range designate the shading you want. (You can designate colors or shadings from 1-7 in intensity). For example, if you have your pie graph's A range designated as cells A1. .F1, you might designate the B range as A2. .F2. Into this second range you would now enter the color shading intensities, 1-7. The first cell in your range would correspond to the first slice of the pie, the second cell, the second slice, and so forth. This is indicated for you in Figure 10.13.

Task — Explode a segment of the pie
Command — SHEET, MENU, GRAPH, 1st SETTING, RANGE
Command — GRAPH, MENU, 1st SETTING, RANGE
Explanation — The EXPLODE commands to separate one or more slices of the pie graph are similar to the commands for shading, outlined previously.

To "explode", follow the shading commands. However, instead of entering numbers 1-7 (for intensities) in the second range, enter the number 100 in each cell that you want exploded outward.

COMPARISON OF SALESPERON'S TOTAL SALES

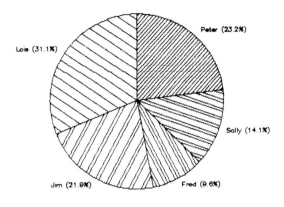

Fig. 10.13 Pie with Shading.

Note: Both shading and exploding can be accomplished by combining numbers. 105 will both shade and explode the slice it refers to. You can see exploded slices of a pie graph in Figure 10.14.

COMPARISON OF SALESPERON'S TOTAL SALES

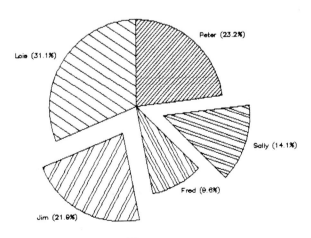

Fig. 10.14 Example of exploded slice of pie.

Task — Squeeze the pie
Command — SHEET, MENU, GRAPH, 2nd SETTING, OTHER, ASPECT
Command — GRAPH, MENU, 2nd SETTING, OTHER, ASPECT
Explanation — This command allows the user to change the shape of the pie. The values which can be set are from .1 (wide) to 10 (narrow). The easiest way to understand this function is to create a pie graph, then try several different aspects and look at the result.

Working With High—Low Graphs

High-low graphs are used for tracking a range of activity. For example, in commodities trading, during an average day the price of wheat or gold will have a high point and a low point. Those highs and lows may in turn be different from the market's opening and closing prices for those commodities. When displaying the day's prices, a range of values is more accurate than individual numbers, hence the use of a high-low scale. Here's an example for gold prices.

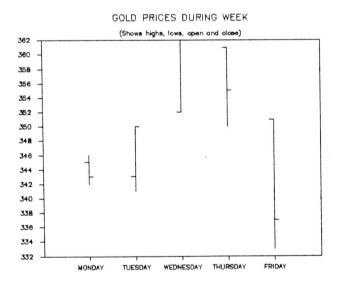

Fig. 10.15 High-Low Values for Gold Prices.

Task — Create a high-low graph
Command — SHEET, MENU, GRAPH, 1st SETTING, TYPE, HIGH-LOW
Command — GRAPH, MENU, 1st SETTING, TYPE, HIGH-LOW
Explanation — Once we've clued Symphony in that we want a high-low graph, it operates the RANGE commands differently. Ranges A-D have special meanings. (Remember, we reach RANGE from GRAPH, 1st SETTING.)

The range settings now operate as follows:

A = Highs

B = Lows

C = Closing price

D = Opening price

Simply enter the appropriate values in cells in your sheet. Then point to those cells for each of the range settings. When you are done you can PREVIEW the completed graph. *Note*: it is not necessary to display all four range settings. You can display only highs and lows if you want, or just the highs alone.

Printing Graphs

Printing your graph should be a relatively simple and painless operation. Unfortunately, it can also be very tricky. The screen prompts tend to be deceptive and sometimes don't really mean what they appear to be saying. However, if you follow the procedure step-by-step, you should have no problems.

Task — Saving a graph so that it can be printed
Command — SHEET, MENU, GRAPH, IMAGE-SAVE
Command — GRAPH, MENU, IMAGE-SAVE
Explanation — As noted earlier, the IMAGE-SAVE command *must* be used. You cannot use SAVE from the SHEET, FILE menu. Also, make sure you do *not* include a suffix in the name.

Task — Use the proper printer
Explanation — Your printer must be capable of graph printing. Typically, this will exclude any daisy wheel printer, but will include most dot matrix printers.

Task — Use the correct installation program
Explanation — When installing Symphony, you were given a series of graphics output devices. You had to select a device and have the installation program copied to the PRINTGRAPH diskette, in order to print out. *Note: to print out you must have selected a printer graphics driver in the install program.*

Task — Use PRINTGRAPH program
Explanation — The graphic printing program for SYMPHONY is handled on a separate program. If you have a two-diskette system, you must insert that diskette into your computer in order to print a graph. If you are using a hard disk drive, you must call up the PRINTGRAPH program. *Note*: in a two-disk system, you may remove your

Symphony diskette to do this. You will normally have your PRINTGRAPH diskette in one drive, and your data diskette with the files to be printed, in the other.

Task — Calling up PRINTGRAPH
Explanation — PRINTGRAPH can be called up in two ways. Either you can select it from the ACCESS MENU (discussed earlier in the book), or you type PGRAPH after the drive prompt on your screen (A > or B >).

Task — Using PRINTGRAPH
Explanation — When you call up PRINTGRAPH you should see a menu. If you have properly installed your printer driver, you will probably be ready to print as soon as you specify the files you want printed.

Task — Calling up graph files to be printed
Command — SETTINGS, HARDWARE, GRAPHS DIRECTORY
Explanation — Although this appears simple, you need to pay attention to what you are doing. Symphony is asking where to locate the files that you want printed out. You need only indicate the drive in which those files are placed. The full drive name should be used, such as A: \ or B: \ .

Enter the location of the files only. *DO NOT* enter the file names. GRAPHPRINT will now search the designated disk and locate only those files which were saved using the IMAGE-SAVE command explained earlier. When you return to the MAIN MENU and select IMAGE, these will be displayed on the screen.

Using the pointer indicate the files you want printed. You can print one file or all of them. After making your selections, enter, and return to the MAIN MENU. Now you're ready to print.

Task — Starting the printer
Command — GO
Explanation — From the MAIN MENU, simply hit the GO command and the printer should begin working.

What If the Printer Won't Print?

Unfortunately, sometimes the printer does nothing when we signal the GO command. After checking that the printer is correctly attached, plugged in, turned on and *on line*, you need to check your hardware settings. They may be incorrect.

Task — Check the interface
Command — SETTINGS, HARDWARE, INTERFACE
Explanation — Symphony offers enormous possibilities for user commands (some say too many!). The INTERFACE command gives you four options: Parallel, Serial, Parallel 2, Serial 2.

Parallel and *serial* are two different ways the signal is transmitted to the printer. If you don't know what they mean, don't worry about it. All that's necessary is that you know which type of transmission your printer uses. Most dot matrix printers use parallel. Most graphic plotters use serial. You may also set the baud rate.

Make the correct selection and be sure your printer is connected to the appropriate serial or parallel port at the back of your computer. (You have a second parallel or serial option as well.)

Task — Check the print driver
Command — SETTINGS, HARDWARE, PRINTER
Explanation — To operate the printer, Symphony must be configured for the printer you have. Symphony offers many different printer drivers in the INSTALL program. You may have selected one or more of these.

When you use the above command, the drivers you have selected can be invoked. Simply choose from those displayed on the screen. *Note*: if you've selected different drivers for different densities, keep in mind that the denser the print-out, the clearer it is and the longer it takes to print.

Task — Set paper to print more than one graph
Command — SETTINGS, ACTION
Explanation — This controls the action you want the printer to take. You are given two choices, PAUSE and EJECT. PAUSE allows you to pause between sheets for single feed paper. EJECT advances the paper after each graph, so you will only end up with one graph per page. This is useful when using form feed paper.

Task — Save the set up commands
Command — SETTINGS, SAVE
Explanation — Once you've set up your printer, you don't want to have to set it up again each time you print. You can prevent this by using the SAVE command. It will save the original selections you made in the SETTINGS MENU.

Customizing the Print-Out

Task — Customizing the print-out
Command — SETTINGS, IMAGE
Explanation — Symphony allows you to customize your print-out with three other controls besides the settings you made when you created your graph. The controls are:

Size
Font
Hue

Let's take them one at a time.

Task — Set the size of the graph
Command — SETTINGS, IMAGE, SIZE
Explanation — The SIZE command allows the graph image to be printed in the following ways:

Full: (a full 8 1/2 by 11-inch page). The graph is printed in sideways rotation, vertically.

Half: (half the normal page size). The graph is printed in the normal fashion on half the page.

Manual: *you* are responsible for setting the left, top, height, width and rotation on the page.

Task — Select the typestyle to be used
Command — SETTINGS, IMAGE, FONT
Explanation — Symphony has 11 *fonts*, that are normally stored on the PRINTGRAPH diskette, and, hence, are readily available. They are displayed when you select the SETTINGS, IMAGE, FONT command. (A font is the alphabet, including numbers and symbols, set in a specific typestyle. Each font is a different style.) The FONT MENU indicates the styles offered.

You can select two different fonts for each graph. The heading is printed in selection 1, the remainder of the text in the other font. The default is BLOCK1, and is used for both heading and text. To make a selection, call up the FONT MENU, select either FONT 1, or FONT 2, and use the pointer to make a selection.

Task — Select the colors to use
Command — SETTINGS, IMAGE, HUE
Explanation — Obviously, this command can only be used with a color plotter or graphics printer, such as the Epson JX-10. It allows you to assign a color to each of the ranges in the graph.

Now you should be ready to enhance your graphs and print them out. There only remains the matter of windowing, which refers to you specifying where you want your graph to be placed on your sheet or document.

CHAPTER 11

Multiple Graphs and Windowing

Thus far we have been dealing with the same *settings*, regardless of the *type* of graph we produced. We created a graph by identifying a range of cells. Then we converted that graph into different types such as line, bar, pie, etc. However, the data which produced each of those graph types remained the same settings with which we began. In other words, we saw different graphic displays of the same information.

This might imply that while Symphony can draw many different types of graphs, the information that produces those graphs must be the same for each.

This is not at all a true picture of Symphony's capabilities. Symphony can produce unlimited numbers of graphs, based on widely different information, all within the framework of a single spreadsheet. An example will clarify this.

Suppose we have the following data in our spreadsheet:

	A	B	C	D	E	F
1	10	20	30	40	50	60
2	9	8	7	6	7	8

We now produce a graph based on the data in the range A1. .F1. A line chart of this data might look like this (Figure 11.1).

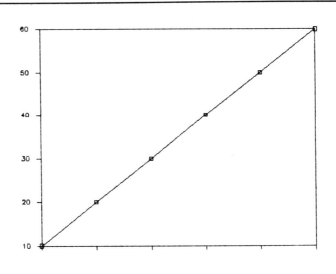

Fig. 11.1 Line Chart Based on First Row.

Two Sets of Information/Two Graphs

We have already seen how we can use the TYPE command to convert this data into a bar, pie or other graph. Now, let's suppose that we want a second graph. But we don't want this second graph to be based on the data in range A1. .AF. Instead, we are going to use the data in range A2. .F2. Essentially, we want two different graphs based on *two different sets of information.*

One way to do this is to go back and change the range in the graph. For example, if we used the A range and gave it the setting of A1. .F1, we can go back and change it to A2. .F2. Now our data will reflect the new information, as will our graphs. However, in creating the new graph data, we will have destroyed the old.

You can circumnavigate this problem by using a second method. When you create a graph it has a settings sheet. (This is similar to our sheet, or data settings sheets.) This sheet specifies the data that makes up the graph. As we've seen, Symphony makes it quite easy to create multiple settings sheets. When you want a graph with information other than what you currently have, instead of replacing the old information with the new, in the current settings sheet, *you can create a new settings sheet.* This allows you to create new graphs with different data, in an almost unlimited fashion, while preserving the data in old graphs. (As we'll see shortly, you can display these different graphs simultaneously on the same screen, and even attach them to parts of your spreadsheet.)

An example will probably clear up any lingering confusion you may have about this. We have already created a settings sheet based on the data in the range A1. .F1. Let's now view that setting sheet. (You can reach it through 1st SETTING, NAME.)

What you are seeing is the 1st SETTING sheet for the graph MAIN. (You can see the second portion of this sheet by switching to 2nd SETTING, but that's not important right now.) Notice that MAIN appears in the lower right hand corner of the sheet, thereby identifying it.

You want to preserve the settings in this sheet while creating a new sheet into which you can put new settings. Using the NAME, CREATE command, type in a new name. (Remember, any name will do, as long as it doesn't have more than 15 characters.) In this case, call it NEWGRAPH. When you enter your new name, presto you have a new sheet!

This can be verified by looking at the lower right hand corner. Instead of the default setting, MAIN, it should now say NEWGRAPH. In addition, if you move to the NAME, USE command, you'll see a directory of two graphs, MAIN and NEWGRAPH. Now different information can be entered in each sheet, producing different graphic displays. (This way you can create as many new sheets as you want.)

It is important to understand, however, that the new sheet you've just created, NEWGRAPH, is not empty. It contains all the information that was in MAIN. You didn't just create a new sheet, you created a new *filled in* sheet. But before it can be used, you must delete the old information and insert new material.

This can be done quickly by selecting the INITIAL SETTINGS command when you're in the NAME MENU. This restores the sheet to the default settings.

In Figure 11.2 you have samples of graphs showing different information.

At this point you can use the RANGE command to enter the new data. In this case, we'll use range A and enter A2. .F2. Now you can preview the two new graphs. You should see bar graphs displaying the data from MAIN and from NEWGRAPH. *Note*: this time we have two of the same type of graphs displaying different information.

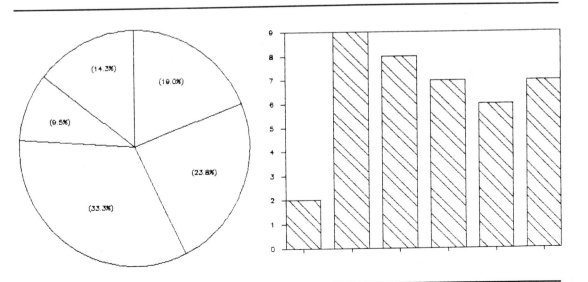

Fig. 11.2 Samples of graphs showing different information.

Windowing

We can create a Symphony window in part of our spreadsheet or document, and attach a graph window to it. (For detailed information on creating a Symphony window see Chapter 8.) In this way, depending on our hardware configuration, we can view one or more graphs through windows at the same time as we see the spreadsheet. (This works only in *shared* mode. If you use *toggle* mode, you can see either graphs or sheet (or document), but not both. See Chapter 2 on installation.)

The procedure is quite simple. From your spreadsheet or document, call up SERVICES, WINDOW, CREATE. Now simply follow the screen prompts. When you are asked what kind of window you want to create, select GRAPH. When you are asked where you want the window to go, display an appropriate part of the screen. (Typically, the lower right hand corner is used for a graph window in a spreadsheet, and either the top or bottom half of the screen is used for a graph in a document window.)

You are then asked to name your window. But you must give it a name other than one currently used. When the information is entered the window will appear on the screen and it will contain the graph MAIN (the default graph name).

An important concept to understand here is the difference between a sheet (or document) window, and a graph window. As we've noted earlier, a window is a view of a particular part of the spreadsheet. If there are two windows open simultaneously, you are viewing two different parts. A sheet window shows a portion of a sheet, exactly as it appears with labels and/or data.

A graph window also shows a portion of the sheet, however, instead of using labels or data, it displays this information in graphic form. Graphs can only be seen through a graph window. However, you can see whatever graphs you want. You can also see the same data on the sheet, and on a graph in a graph window, simultaneously.

Any graph can be attached to a graph window. For example, let's say you wanted to view the graph, NEWGRAPH. You just created it in the window you just opened.

To accomplish this, you use the SERVICES, WINDOW, USE command to call up the graphic window. *Once the graph window is the current window*, hit the MENU key. Instead of the usual MENU, the GRAPH MENU will be displayed. Now hit the first command, which is ATTACH. You will now be given a choice of which graph you want to attach to this window. You can choose MAIN, NEWGRAPH, or any other that has been created.

In this manner you can *thumb through* the various graphs and insert them in your window.

Multiple Graph Windows

Multiple graph windows can be created by going through the procedure just indicated above. However, instead of opening only one window, we can open several. (If you are unsure about this, reread Chapter 8 on windows.)

The graph windows can be overlapping or side-by-side. You can call up any graph settings sheet in any graph window, by first, making that window active, second, using the ATTACH command while in the graph window, and third, selecting your choice.

Windowing Tasks

The following material presents the concepts of windowing and graphs which was just discussed, in the **Task/Command/Explanation** format. This gives you an easy reference for specific tasks that you need to review. *Note*: the following commands can be reached *either* through SHEET, MENU, GRAPH, or GRAPH, MENU.

Task — Create a new graph settings sheet
Command — 1st SETTING, NAME, CREATE
Explanation — To create another settings sheet, simply use the commands indicated above, and then write in a new name (up to 15 characters). Instantly a new sheet will appear. *Note*: the new sheet will have the exact same settings as the old. You will need to remove the old settings and put in new ones.

Task — Remove the old settings from a new graph settings sheet
Command — 1st SETTING, NAME, INITIAL SETTING
Command — 1st SETTING, CANCEL
Explanation — The INITIAL SETTING command will reset all the settings to their default. The CANCEL command will give you the option of selectively cancelling settings. The selections under CANCEL are: ENTIRE-ROW, RANGE, FORMAT, DATA-LABELS, LEGEND, HUE.

Task — Create new settings in new graph setting sheet
Command — 1st SETTING, RANGE
Explanation — Once you've removed the old settings from a new sheet, add in the new settings in the same way you would when creating any new graph.

Task — Create a graph window
Command — SERVICES, WINDOW, CREATE, NAME, TYPE, AREA
Explanation — As soon as you get to CREATE, in the above string of commands, you can begin thinking about the specific graphic window you want to create. CREATE will ask you to give a new name to your window. Any name can be selected, but one that is descriptive, such as GRAPH1 usually helps.

As soon as you enter the name you'll be asked the type of window to create. Select GRAPH. Next the screen will display inverse type and you'll be asked the area you want to designate for your window. Use the pointer keys to indicate where the window is to appear on the screen. (The pointer (cursor) is oriented at the bottom right of the screen. If you want to orient it at the top right, hit the period key until it moves around to the top, anchoring it there.)

Finally, you will be asked if you want to *restrict* or otherwise *modify* the window. No command is required here. Using [**ESC**] several times will return you to the active window, which will now be the graph window you have created. Your graph should now be displayed.

Task — Display a different graph in a graph window
Command — GRAPH (must use a GRAPH environment here) MENU, ATTACH
Explanation — When you are in a graph window, you can select the MENU, ATTACH command. This will immediately call up a directory of all of the graph setting sheets you've selected. You can now point to the settings sheet you want displayed. When you enter your selection, the appropriate graph will appear.

Task — Create multiple windows with graphics in each
Explanation — This requires an understanding of both windowing and graph settings sheets. To create multiple windows, reread Chapter 8 on windows. Put simply, this task means you want to create new windows in different sections of the screen. Be sure each window in which you want to place a graph is a *graph window type*.

To get different graphs in each window, make each graph window active. When a window is active, select the MENU, ATTACH command. This will display the various graph settings sheets that are available. Simply make your selection and that graph will appear in that window. Then go on and make the next window active, and continue until all windows display the graphs you want to see.

Task — Display both graph and sheet (or document) on the same screen
Explanation — This will occur automatically, if you are in either a SHEET or DOC environment and create a graph window smaller than the full size of the screen. But you *must* have selected the shared mode (and have a graphics monitor and board) when you installed Symphony. If you selected the toggle mode, you can see either graphs or sheet (or document), but not both together. You will have to toggle back and forth between them.

Task — Change graph by changing spreadsheet
Explanation — This is done automatically. Each time you change the data on which the graph is based, the graph itself will update. This can be quite dramatic in the shared mode. You can display the data on which the graph is based on one part of the screen, and the graph in a window on another part. You can then change the data and watch the graph update. In this way you can try out different graphic presentations in a "what if" manner.

Task — Keep graph constant while changing worksheet
Command — SERVICES, WINDOW, SETTINGS, AUTO-DISPLAY
Explanation — Selecting the NO option here will stop the automatic updating of the graph. The graph will remain fixed as it was in the last update, regardless of changes you may make in the underlying spreadsheet. To get the graph to update after you've turned off the AUTO-DISPLAY, use the DRAW key [**ALT**] plus [**F8**].

CHAPTER
12

Introduction
to Symphony's
Data Base

Many people who begin working on a computerized data base for the first time have little more than a vague idea of what it is. They almost always have an excellent idea of what they want to accomplish with it, however.

For example, you are a business owner. You have inventory and you want to maintain accurate records of the items you are carrying. You want to be able to quickly find out how much stock you have of a particular item, where it's located or from who you ordered it.

Or perhaps you have a series of addresses that you want to be able to print out by zip code, name, state or any other sorting.

Maybe you are responsible for a large number of employees. You want to keep track of their personnel data, as well as their salaries. You want to be able to know how many employees are earning above or below a certain amount, or how many are on the administrative staff and how many are on the sales staff. You also want to print out checks each pay period.

Or there might be yet some other use for a data base. As you can see, there are many tasks that can be performed. You really don't need to know exactly what a data base is when you start working with it. You'll acquire that knowledge as you go along.

To begin, however, let's use a broad definition. A data base is usually a large amount of information that you want to put into a particular order, and then, sometimes to print out in a special form. Symphony's *data base manager* does just that. It "manages" the data for you.

Your Responsibilities

Of course, Symphony can't do it all alone. It has to have vital information that only you can provide. This information is divided into three categories:

1. The *form* in which the data is to be entered. (In a later chapter we'll see how to enter data without a form.)

2. The *data* itself.

3. The *instructions* to Symphony, explaining how you want the data manipulated.

For example, let's say you want to create an index for a book such as this. The easiest way is to (1) create a form in which you will enter the data (called an entry form). (2) Enter the data (the items to be indexed) itself. Finally, (3) tell Symphony specifically what you want it to do with that data (such as alphabetize). Figure 12.1 shows the progression from entry to print-out.

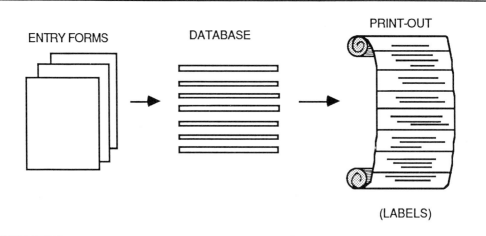

ENTRY FORMS   DATABASE   PRINT-OUT

(LABELS)

Fig. 12.1 Flow Chart of Entry Form - Data Base - Print-Out.

In this chapter, we'll concentrate on creating a form and entering data. Then, in the next chapter, we'll learn how to manipulate that data to get out the information we want. And finally, we'll see how to work directly from a SHEET environment and print out reports and labels.

What Symphony Can Do

Before we get started, however, let's take a moment to discuss what Symphony can do. Symphony *can work with several data bases simultaneously*. It *can store an enormous amount of information* in a data base (up to the size of the underlying spreadsheet and the memory of your computer). It *can create the entry form* for you with only a minimum amount of information supplied to it. Also, the basics of its operation *can be learned in only a few minutes*, yet it is sufficiently complex to handle almost any data base chore.

Getting Started

I'm going to assume you've never worked with a data base and have no idea what it is, or even what it looks like. Perhaps you're even a bit intimidated by it. (If you've browsed through Symphony, you may have come across the *form* window used in data base management. You probably noticed that it's blank, and that apparently it can't be entered by typing. That alone can be intimidating. Relax! In a few minutes you'll be running a data base like a pro.)

Fields and Records

The essence of a data base is composed of *fields* and *records*. A field is like a heading, it is the label under which specific items are listed. The record is the specific listing of an item. It's helpful to think of fields as columns on a spreadsheet, with a heading at the top, and records as each row of that spreadsheet. For example, in the following form can you identify the fields and the record?

NAME	ADDRESS
John Jones	123 West Main St.
Sally Smith	456 Main Ave.

The headings of the columns are Name and Address. They are the fields, the items that are going to appear on *every* form. The specific data, in this case, John Jones, and 123 West Main St., the rows, will occur only once. They are considered the record. If it still isn't clear, any confusion should vanish when you create an entry form. We'll do that now with Symphony's help.

Employee Record Entry Forms

Assume that you are in personnel, and you want to keep track of employees and their salaries. You need to begin by organizing the information you want to keep on each employee.

Perhaps you want the following:

NAME
ADDRESS
CITY
STATE
ZIP
DATE EMPLOYED
STARTING SALARY
CURRENT SALARY

The old-fashioned way to keep track of this information was to write it out on a 3 x 5 card. With a computer, however, instead of a 3 x 5 card, you will be using an *entry form*, that you will have created on the screen.

Creating the Entry Form

You need to begin in the SHEET environment. (Symphony's data base utilizes three environments, SHEET, FORM and DOC. We'll use all three in this chapter.) Simply enter the information you want on each employee in the A column of the spreadsheet. (It's a good idea to start with a new spreadsheet if this is your first experience with a data base.)

```
————————A————————————B————————

1 NAME:L
2 ADDRESS:L
3 CITY:L
4 STATE:L
5 ZIP:L
6 DATE EMPLOYED:D
7 STARTING SALARY:N
8 CURRENT SALARY:N
```

Notice that after each entry, there is an L, D, or N. You use these letters to tell Symphony to treat the entries as:

L = Label
D = Date
N = Number

Two other entries are T for time, and C for compute. (More will be said about these later.) As soon as the information is entered, switch to the FORM environment. Don't panic if the FORM is blank. At this stage it should be. In the upper left hand corner you will see the message, "(No Definition range defined)". In essence, Symphony is telling you to define the entry form. (Remember, the entry form is our means of putting information into our data base.) We'll do that now.

From the FORM MENU, hit MENU, GENERATE. This tells Symphony to generate a form. It will then ask a series of questions:

LABEL NUMBER DATE TIME COMPUTED — this is asking for the type of entry you've made. Since you've already indicated this with a colon and letter after each entry, just hit [ENTER] to get to the next question. (Notice that the default setting is LABEL.)

DEFAULT FIELD LENGTH — this is asking how much space you need in which to write the data on the form. The default is 9, but you will want a lot of room, so enter 20 characters.

NAME — Symphony wants a name for the data base. For this example, enter DATA1

RANGE OF FIELD LENGTH — this is the most important question. Symphony is asking for the fields that will make up your entry form. Of course, you've already created them on your SHEET. SYMPHONY returns you to the sheet, and all you have to do is highlight the items you've already listed (A1. .A8).

That's it! To see your entry form, just hit [ENTER]. It should appear on your screen as shown below:

```
Inserting Record 1                 New Record                              FORM
Enter NAME
NAME    _____
ADDRESS _____
CITY    _____
STATE   _____
ZIP     _____
DATE EMPLOYED   _____
STARTING SALARY _____
CURRENT SALARY  _____
```

Fig. 12.2 Diagram of Entry Form.

Entering Data in the Entry Form

Now that you've created your entry form, it's time to try it out. Begin by entering the data for one of the employees. You will be guided by a message in the upper left hand corner. The first field is NAME. Enter Peter Jones for the name. Now hit [ENTER]. The cursor moves down to the next item and you get a new prompt in the upper left hand corner of your screen.

You make an entry, or choose to skip this field. If you make a mistake, you can use [BACKSPACE]. Each time you hit [ENTER], or the [LEFT ARROW] or the [DOWN

ARROW], the cursor will move to a new entry. In this way you will be coached to make an entry on each line. (When you get to the bottom line, the cursor will jump back up to the top.) For now skip down to the DATE line. Notice that like other fields, it has room for 20 characters. This is the setting you chose earlier.

The date must be entered in one of two forms. Either 03/12/86 *or* 03-DEC-86. Because you indicated that this would be a date entry, Symphony will "beep" if you do not enter a date.

Moving down to the first salary line, you must now enter a value (not a label). Symphony will beep if you try to enter a label. *Note*: if you had specified that this field was to be a (L)abel field, you could have entered numbers. But then the numbers would be treated as words. They couldn't be added, subtracted and so forth. Because you have entered them as values you can perform all the usual mathematical functions with them.

When you have finished making as many entries as you want on this form, hit the INSERT key ([**INS**]). (Symphony may beep as you hit [**INS**]. It is telling you that you haven't finished with the last entry. Just hit [**ENTER**], then [**INS**].) This enters the record you've just created into your data base and pops a new entry form onto the screen. You can tell you are in a new record because the words NEW RECORD will appear at the top center of the screen. You can now fill out the second record of your personnel data base.

About Records and Fields

The distinction between records and fields should be a bit more clear now. Each time you finish entering all the data concerning a particular employee you have completed a single record. You enter this into your data base, and a new form then pops up in which you can enter data about another employee. However, on all the forms, the headings or questions remain constant. These are the *fields*.

More Records

Assuming you have created an entry form such as the one just described, continue making entries until you have four or five completed records. The following steps should prove helpful.

Task — Insert a record
Explanation — Hit the INSERT key ([**INS**]).

Task — See a previous record
Explanation — Hit the [**PAGE UP**].

Task — See a later record
Explanation — Hit [**PAGE DOWN**].

You can now create an entry record, and move backward and forward through your entries.

Task — Edit data in a record
Explanation — Use the [**ARROW**] keys or [**ENTER**] to move through the fields until you get to the one you want changed. To change an entire entry, just type the new entry. The old one will disappear. To change a single letter or value, hit the EDIT key ([**F2**] and move the cursor to the area to be changed. Hit [**DELETE**], then add the new character(s).

A Review

Before we proceed with some advanced forms, let's take just a moment to review what we've done. We've created *a form* on which to enter data. We've entered *data*. And we've learned how to move back and forth in our *records*.

Now, let's consider what we have *not* done. We haven't yet seen an actual data base, nor have we learned how to manipulate it. We'll tackle the manipulating in the next chapter. For now, however, let's take a glance at our actual data base to see where it is and what it looks like. To do this, just switch from the FORM environment to the SHEET environment. You should see something like Figure 12.3.

You will probably recognize several things here. At the top is the material you entered into the sheet originally (now called the *definition range*), and below that is the form Symphony created for us (called the *entry range*). Now look at the very bottom of the sheet. There you'll see the data base range. That's the actual data base itself.

All the items on this sheet, with the exception of the original material in the definition range, and the data, were created by Symphony in order to set up the data base for us. Don't be intimidated by the sheet Symphony has created. It's not hard to understand, and in the next chapters you'll be manipulating it like a pro.

Changing the Entry Form

Perhaps you felt that the entry form we created with all the entries on the left hand side, was a bit awkward. Indeed it was, however, when Symphony creates the form for us, that's the way it comes out. But the form can easily be changed. This is done in the SHEET environment. Turn there now and locate the section that displays the entry form as it appears in the sheet window (Figure 12.4).

Now, switch to a DOC environment. You'll recall that at the onset, I said that Symphony used three environments for data base. We have thus far worked in FORM and SHEET. Now we'll try our hand at DOC.

Using the word processing commands available in the DOC environment, edit this form. *Note: you must first turn off automatic justification or your form will be thrown off.* (Use MENU, FORMAT, SETTINGS, JUSTIFICATION NONE).

```
          -----A--------B--------C----D---E-----F--------G---------H--------I-----
   1   NAME:L
   2   ADDRESS:L
   3   CITY:L
   4   STATE:L
   5   ZIP:L
   6   DATE EMPLOYED:D
   7   STARTING SALARY:N
   8   CURRENT SALARY:N
   9
  10   NAME
  11   ADDRESS
  12   CITY
  13   STATE
  14   ZIP
  15   DATE EMPLOYED
  16   STARTING SALARY
  17   CURRENT SALARY
  18
  19   Name    Value   Type DefauForValidity Input  Prompt
  20   NAME             L:9                          Enter NAME
  21   ADDRESS          L:9                          Enter ADDRESS
  22   CITY             L:9                          Enter CITY
  23   STATE            L:9                          Enter STATE
  24   ZIP              L:9                          Enter ZIP
  25   DATE EMPLOYED    D:9                          Enter DATE EMPLOYED
  26   STARTING SALARY  N:9                          Enter STARTING SALA
  27   CURRENT SALARY   N:9                          Enter CURRENT SALAR
  28
  29   NAME    ADDRESS  CITY STATEZIPDATE EMPLOSTARTING SCURRENT SALARY
  30
  31
  32   NAME    ADDRESS  CITY STATEZIPDATE EMPLOSTARTING SCURRENT SALARY
  33
  34
  35
  36
  37   NAME    ADDRESS  CITY STATEZIPDATE EMPLOSTARTING SCURRENT SALARY
  38
  39
  40
```

FIELDS (rows 1–8)
ENTRY RANGE (rows 10–17)
DEFINITION RANGE (rows 19–27)
MAIN REPORT RANGE (rows 29–30)
CRITERION RANGE (rows 32–33)
DATA BASE (rows 37–...)

Note: In the above chart several of the columns have been compressed to make viewing easier.

Fig. 12.3 Sheet showing data references labelled according to what they are.

```
B10:                                                                      SHEET

------------------------A----------------B-------------------C---------------┐
1                       NAME:L
2                       ADDRESS:L
3                       CITY:L
4                       STATE:L
5                       ZIP:L
6                       DATE EMPLOYED:D
7                       STARTING SALARY:N
8                       CURRENT SALARY:N
9
10                      NAME _____
11                      ADDRESS _____
12                      CITY _____
13                      STATE _____
14                      ZIP _____
15                      DATE EMPLOYED _____
16                      STARTING SALARY _____
17                      CURRENT SALARY _____
18
19                      Name                Value
20                      NAME
                        ADDRESS
15-Jan-85   12:53 AM                                             Cap
```

Fig. 12.4 Illustration of that portion of sheet which has entry form.

You should have no difficulty when you follow these general guidelines:

1. Make any adjustments to length of line by using *underline* while the form is still *flush left*. If you shorten lines, the form will appear different, however the same number of characters may still be set as per your original setting. (In our case it was 20.)

2. Use the MOVE command to change the relation of one field to another.

3. Do not put more than 78 characters on any line, including fields, names and underlining.

4. Do not change the *order* of the fields. They must read the same as the *entry definitions*; that is, from top to bottom and left to right. You can, however, move lower fields to upper lines. (This should be a consideration when you originally create the form.)

5. Do not delete or leave out a field. Every field that you put in the entry range must also appear in the definition range.

You can shrink some lines and make others longer, in other words, be creative. Here's a sample of a redesigned form.

NAME _____

ADDRESS _____

CITY _____STATE _____ZIP _____

DATE _____STARTING SALARY _____

CURRENT SALARY _____

Inserting the Newly Designed Form

When you switch back to the *form window*, your new form should appear. In some cases, however, it may not. Instead, you'll get a message which reads, "Entry/Definition ranges mismatched". This simply means that you've outgrown the bounds of the entry range you defined when you created the form. Now go back and enlarge the entry area to accommodate your new form. You can do this on the *form settings sheet* found through FORM, MENU, SETTINGS, FORM ENTRY. Highlight the correct block and you'll be on your way. (We'll learn much more about the settings sheet in the next chapter.)

Modifications

It is possible to further modify the entry form. We can limit the kinds of entries that can be made, we can insert formulas, we can even customize the prompts that occur on the top left of our screen when we enter records.

These modifications are best made from a SHEET environment, where we can see exactly what we are doing. If you go there now you'll see that Symphony has constructed our data base and its various ranges. We are going to be particularly concerned with the *definition range*, as shown in Figure 12.5.

```
J18:                                                                    SHEET
     ----A----B------C-----D--------E------F--------G-------H---------------------
18
19   Name    Value   Type   Default Formula Validity Input Prompt
20   NAME            L:20                                   Enter NAME
21   ADDRESS         L:20                                   Enter ADDRESS
22   CITY            L:20                                   Enter CITY
23   STATE           L:20                                   Enter STATE
24   ZIP             L:20                                   Enter ZIP
25   DATE EMPLOYEDD:20                                      Enter DATE EMPLOYED
26   STARTING SALAN:20                                      Enter STARTING SALARY
27   CURRENT SALARN:20                                      Enter CURRENT SALARY
38
39
30
31
32
33
34
35
```

Fig. 12.5 Illustration of Definition Range.

The definition range "defines" what happens to the material we enter into the form. It uses eight columns for this. We'll modify the form by working with these columns. They are:

Name   Value   Type   Default   Formula   Validity   Input   Prompt

Some of the columns are merely work places for Symphony, and we'll have no specific use for them. However, to help in understanding the whole picture, we'll go through each one. Let's start from the right hand side and proceed left. (This is not the way Symphony handles information. However, by coming in the back door, we will be better able to see the uses of the different ranges.)

Prompts

Task — Change the prompts
Explanation — The *prompt* tells Symphony what prompt to put up in the left hand window when the cursor is on a field. The default prompts are simply the field names we have chosen. This means that in our example on fields in the last chapter, the first field which we called Name is also the prompt. When we get to the name line on the entry form, Symphony asks "Name?" in the upper left hand corner. However, the prompts can be customized.

Perhaps, instead of just bringing up "NAME," we'd like Symphony to say at the first field, "Please write your name here." To accomplish this, we just type in the prompt we want and it will replace the default that Symphony supplied.

Input

This is Symphony's work column. It uses the particular cells in this location to process information that we input. *Don't write in these cells.*

Validity

Task — Check the value entries made in the form
Explanation — Symphony allows us to create a *validity test* for each value field. If the data entered doesn't pass the test, Symphony won't allow it to be entered. Typically, this type of test asks if the value is greater than, or less than, a particular number.

For example, a company may have a dividing line in terms of salaries. Those making more than $20,000 per year are considered management, those making less are considered support staff. This particular data base may pertain only to the support staff. How can we be sure that we don't inadvertantly include someone from management?

A validity test on current salary, (allowing only entries under $20,000) can be made. It would look like this:

+ B27 < 20000

This entry would go into cell F27. It says that before Symphony can allow the data to be entered, the value in cell B27 (the value cell for current salary) must be less than 20,000. If it's more, Symphony will beep and refuse the entry.

Formula

Task — Have a formula operate on data entered into the form
Explanation — We can create a formula that will operate on either values or labels. It goes in the *formula* column. Symphony will read this column, and then perform the calculation, before displaying the result in the form window.

For example, perhaps we want the starting salary in our current form to be shown as a percentage of a standard base salary that the company offers (let's use $10,000 as a base salary). When we enter the field name, Starting Salary, we should make it a C type, for Compute. That way, instead of simply inserting the value typed, Symphony will first compute it on the basis of a formula we enter. Our formula might look like this:

+ B26/X1

B26 would represent the value entered for current salary. X1 would represent a cell which contained the value, 10000. When Symphony came to the current salary, it would always divide by cell X1, or 10,000. The result would be expressed on the form as a decimal between 0 and 2. In the formula column, then, we can make reference to cells either in the definition range or outside of it, and to absolute or to relative values.

Default

Task — Create a ready made entry for one or more fields
Explanation — Sometimes it is convenient to have an entry already listed in a field. If it's incorrect, the user can write over it. But if it's correct, then it saves having to make a new entry.

For example, one of the fields in our form was State. Chances are, however, that nearly all the employees will be from the same state (assuming we're dealing with a single plant). Therefore, you could write "Calif." or "New York" whatever the appropriate state is in the default column in the row corresponding to the State field. Now, each time the form comes up, the state will already be listed. In the event that it is the wrong state, you need only type in the correct one to change it.

Type

Task — Change the type of field or the entry length in the form

Explanation — We have already seen that there are five different types of field entries: Label, Number, Date, Time and Compute. Under the *type* heading, we indicate the type of field we are dealing with. If we want to change the type we can do it here.

In addition, there is also a number after the type. In this case, the number is 20. This stands for the length of the entry space measured in characters. You'll recall we set 20 when we generated the form. However, we can change the length for each field to other numbers.

Value Range

Explanation — The *Value Range* is where Symphony stores values input after it has been processed.

Name Range

Explanation — The names used in the fields are displayed under the *Name* heading. You can change them, however, they *must* correspond identically in location and spelling to the names in the entry range.

Summary

Now we have enough information to create and modify a form for entering information to a data base. Let's see what we can do about excerpting information once that data base has been created.

CHAPTER
13

Getting
Information Out
of Your Data Base

In the last chapter we went into detail about how to create a form that would allow us to insert information into a data base. Now, we are going to get some practice at accessing information from a data base.

There are two ways to access and manipulate a data base. The first is through a FORM environment, the second is through a SHEET environment. Using a FORM environment is easiest, and we will concentrate on that method in this chapter. The next chapter will explore ways to use the SHEET environment, for those who want greater versatility and challenge.

Working in a Form Environment

There are essentially two goals that you need to accomplish in the FORM environment. The first is matching, which means getting Symphony to pull out a particular record, or group of records. The second goal is to sort the data base in a different way than you would otherwise. *Note*: throughout this chapter I'm going to assume you've read the previous chapter and have created a data base similar to the one described there. I'll be referring to that data base from time to time.

♯ulling Out Selected Records

You accomplish this by telling Symphony the particular characteristic(s) of the records you want to select. For example, maybe you want to only see those records for people who live in New Mexico. Or perhaps you want to only see the records of items of which you have more than 15 in stock. The selection process is virtually limitless. All that is required is that you tell Symphony the *criteria* you want to use to make the selection.

Task — Choose the criteria for making a selection
Command — FORM, MENU, CRITERIA, EDIT
Explanation — When you issue this command, you will be shown a blank entry form that looks like this:

```
Editing Criterion Record 1 of 1                                    CRIT
Enter NAME
NAME  _____
ADDRESS  _____
CITY _____
STATE _____
ZIP _____
DATE EMPLOYED _____
STARTING SALARY _____
CURRENT SALARY _____
```

Fig. 13.1 Blank Entry Form.

You'll notice that this form is different from your regular entry form, in that it says CRIT at the upper right hand corner. Also, at the left it says, "Editing Criteria Record 1 of 1".

This is a criteria entry form, on which you enter the criteria you want to use to select different records from your data base. For example, if you write New Mexico in the *field* for State, that tells Symphony you *only* want to see those records in your data base which have New Mexico as the state.

Or, you could have entered Jones, $10,000 and New Mexico. Symphony would now only pull the record(s) that exactly matched those criteria. But for now, let's just designate the state as the only criteria you have.

Insert the criteria by hitting **[INS]** (in the same manner as you did for entering a regular form.)

Now hit **[PAGE UP]**. You're back to the familiar entry form.

Task — View the records selected by the criteria
Command — FORM, MENU, CRITERIA, USE
Explanation — If you want to see all the records you have entered that have New Mexico as the state, simply go back to FORM, MENU, CRITERIA. This time, however, instead of EDIT, select USE. The screen will look like this:

```
Editing Record 2 of 15 (1 Match)                          FORM
Enter NAME
NAME John Smith_____
ADDRESS 23 Elm St._____
CITY Albuquerque_____
STATE New Mexico_____
ZIP _____
DATE EMPLOYED 12/5/81_____
STARTING SALARY 12000_____
CURRENT SALARY 15400_____
```

Fig. 13.2 Criteria Match Screen.

Again, we have FORM in the upper right hand corner, but the message (editing record 2 of 15) tells you that you are actually viewing only the second record out of a total of 15. This is the only match which has New Mexico as a state. If there were other matching records it would say something such as "Match 1 of 3". To see the next matching record we would use [**PAGE DOWN**]. *Note*: as you go through each of these records, they are automatically dumped back into the data base. When you finish viewing the last record, you can use CRITERIA, IGNORE to return to the entry form.

Task — Change an entry that has been selected
Command — FORM, MENU, CRITERIA, USE
Explanation — When you see the matches, Symphony automatically puts you in the EDIT mode. Just type in any changes you want, and they will be made on the record that is dumped back into the data base.

Task — Create multiple criteria for the same field
Command — FORM, MENU, CRITERIA, EDIT
Explanation — Suppose you wanted to select those people named Jones, and those named Smith, who lived in New Mexico. You would call up the criteria entry form using the above commands. On the initial form you would enter Jones for the name, and New Mexico for the state. However, instead of returning to the data base, you would now go to a second criteria card by hitting [**PAGE DOWN**]. (The screen will say, "Inserting Criterion Record 2.")

When you've reached this point, then type in Smith for the name, and New Mexico for the state and hit [**ENTER**]. Then use [**PAGE UP**] until you get to the regular entry mode. Symphony will now display those records in which Smith, New Mexico and Jones, New Mexico are written.

Task — Locate "guessed" records
Command — ?, *, @FIND, @LEFT, @EXACT
Explanation — Sometimes we want Symphony to search through the data base to find a name of which we are unsure of the spelling. There are several methods of accomplishing this.

? — This can be used to match *any* letter in a field position. For example, you want to find the records for those living in Simi. However, you are not sure of the spelling of the word. After the State field, you can enter "Sim?". Symphony will now match Sim and any other letter.

You can also use the ? with zip codes, provided you have specified that they are (L)abel entries and not (N)umber entries.

* — This can be used to fill in a word. Placed after any string in a label, it will match that string with any suffix. For example, Sim* would match Sim with any suffixes that followed, including Simi, Simy and Simpleton.

@**FIND, @LEFT, @EXACT** — These functions, as well as formulas, can be entered directly through the criteria form window. Their operations are identical to the way they perform on a SHEET. Check into Chapter 7 for a further explanation of each of these.

Task — Get out of the criteria mode
Command — FORM, MENU, CRITERIA, IGNORE
Explanation — This turns off *matching*.

Task — Change, or use different criteria
Command — FORM, MENU, CRITERIA, EDIT
Command — FORM, MENU, SETTINGS, NAME, CREATE
Explanation — Suppose that you have created a set of criteria to select forms. Now you want to change that criteria to something totally different. For example, instead of matching by salary or state, you want matches by name and city, with no regard for salary or state.

There are two methods of changing the criteria you are using. One method is to go back and re-edit your criteria form, inserting new criteria in the fields.

The second is to create a new settings sheet, with different criteria on it. The settings sheets, you'll recall from the chapters on the SHEET environment, contain the settings used in the current window, in this case in the current *form* window.

Creating a new settings sheet is valuable because it allows you to keep the original criteria, in case you want to use it again in the future. You reach the settings sheet from the FORM, MENU, SETTINGS commands. (An example of the sheet follows.)

Figure 13.3 is a *form settings sheet*. Note that both the data base and the criterion range are listed in the top left hand corner. Our goal is to create a new settings sheet into which we can then *input* a new criterion range.

```
Database, Criterion, Output ranges                                    MENU
Basic  Form  Underscores  Sort-Keys  Report  One-Record  Name  Cancel  Quit

 ┌──────────────────────────────────────────────────────────────────────────┐
 │ Basic Ranges                         Report Ranges                         │
 │   Database:                            Main:                               │
 │   Criterion:                           Above:                              │
 │   Output:                              Below:                              │
 │ Form Ranges                            Type          Single                │
 │   Entry:                               Entry list:                         │
 │   Definition:                          Input cell:                         │
 │ Underscores:       Yes                 One-Record:       No                │
 │ Sort-Keys                                                                  │
 │   1st-Key:              2nd-Key:                     3rd-Key:              │
 │     Order:                Order:                       Order:             │
 │                                            ──Database Settings: MAIN╳      │
 └──────────────────────────────────────────────────────────────────────────┘
```

Fig. 13.3 Settings Sheet.

Create a New Settings Sheet

This is easily accomplished using the NAME, CREATE from the FORM MENU. The
process of creating a new form settings sheet is similar to that of creating a new *sheet*
settings sheet, described in an earlier chapter.

   Give the new settings sheet a name (call it BCRIT). The new BCRIT settings sheet is
now in existence. It will be identical to the original, however. You should now create a
new criterion range right on your worksheet (see next chapter).

   Now use the SETTINGS, BASIC, CRITERION commands to highlight the new
range and it will become part of the sheet.

Attach the New Settings Sheet

This is accomplished using the FORM, MENU, ATTACH command. Symphony will
now display on the screen all the data base settings sheets that have been created. *Main*
is the sheet you originally started in. BCRIT should also be listed. Point to BCRIT and hit
[ENTER]. Now your new settings sheet is attached to your data base. Input the new
criteria according to the procedure described above, and it can then be used to select
records from the data base.

   You can *delete* the new or any other settings sheet by using the FORM, SETTINGS,
NAME, DELETE command.

   Note: settings sheets can also be used to create new criterion, entry ranges or even
sortings (described below).

Task — Switch to other settings sheets
Command — FORM, MENU, ATTACH
Explanation — When you use the ATTACH command you will be shown an alphabetical list of all the different form settings sheets you've created. Simply list the one
you want.

≣Sort/Resort Your Data Base

Now that we've seen how we can pull out records from a data base, the next goal is to learn how to sort the data base so that you can get it arranged the way you want it. For example, I recently created a book index. All the headings were entered into an entry form. When that was completed, I had created a data base which consisted of all the headings used in the book. They had been entered as they appeared in the text.

An index, however, requires an alphabetical arrangement. So I used Symphony's sorting ability to instantly sort all the headings, sub-headings, and sub-sub headings so that they were alphabetized.

Of course, you may never need to index a book, but you may need to alphabetize your data base. Or, you may need to sort an inventory by date, so that the last entries appear first. At some point you may need to sort addresses so they are in order by zip code. Whatever your sorting chore, chances are Symphony can accomplish it.

Task — Sort the data base
Command — FORM, MENU, SETTINGS, SORT-KEY
Explanation — In order to sort the data base, we must use the settings sheet. This is reached by the commands noted above. Here is a settings sheet for the data base we have constructed:

```
Database, Criterion, Output ranges                                    MENU
Basic  Form  Underscores  Sort-Keys  Report  One-Record  Name  Cancel  Quit
┌─────────────────────────────────────────────────────────────────────────┐
│ Basic Ranges                           Report Ranges                      │
│   Database:      MAIN_DB                  Main:         MAIN_MA            │
│   Criterion:     MAIN_CR                  Above:        MAIN_AB            │
│   Output:                                 Below:                          │
│ Form Ranges                               Type          Single            │
│   Entry:         MAIN_EN                    Entry list:                    │
│   Definition:    MAIN_DF                    Input cell:                    │
│ Underscores:     Yes                    One-Record:     No                 │
│ Sort-Keys                                                                  │
│   1st-Key:                2nd-Key:                  3rd-Key:               │
│     Order:                  Order:                    Order:               │
└───────────────────────────────────────────Database Settings: MAIN⟩───────┘
```

Fig. 13.4 Settings Sheet.

The settings sheet gives you the basic information on your form. You probably noticed that it lists the ranges that your data base occupies on the sheet, as well as those that your criteria (if any) occupy. The bottom of the settings sheet lists three *sort keys*. This is where sorting takes place.

To begin, select SORT-KEY from the SETTINGS MENU. You are now given a selection of three keys. Each one will sort a different field of the data base. Up to three keys can be used simultaneously. Let's begin by sorting the data base by the current salaries of employees.

```
A72:                                                          SHEET


------------------------------H------------------------
  10                    CURRENT  SALARY
  11                    13500
  12                    15400
  13                    12950
  14                    13590
  15                    12500
  16                    21750
  17                    42000
  18                    14500
  19                    37900
  20                    30000
                        15500
                        14500
                        13000
                        12900
                        16000
```

Fig. 13.5 Sheet Showing Data Base Fields.

Select the first sort key. Symphony immediately returns you to the SHEET and asks for the data base and the field to be sorted. An example of this sheet is offered in Figure 13.5.

Now point to the column of the field to be sorted. In this case, it is the column headed by "Current Salary." You're asked if you want the data base sorted in (A)scending or (D)escending order.

Ascending means that the letter A, or the highest number, will be first. *Descending* means that the letter W, or the lowest number, will be first. Make your selection. (When you are combining letters and numbers, Symphony will sort according to the selection of numbers first, or letters first, that you made when you installed the program.)

If there are duplicates, then the second number or letter of the string will be used as a tie breaker, then the third, and so forth. Once you have selected the order you are returned to the MENU. The data base can now be sorted by selecting MENU, RECORD-SORT. When you press this you are asked if you want the data base sorted by "Unique" or "All." "All" sorts all records, "Unique" eliminates duplicates. *Note*: if we select "Unique," every field in both duplicate records must match, in order for the duplicate to be eliminated. As soon as you make your selection, Symphony will complete the sort. You can then browse through the new sorting via the form window.

Task — Sort more than one field
Command — FORM, MENU, SETTINGS, SORT KEYS
Explanation — The 1st sort key receives the most use. Only when there are duplicates in the first sort key field will the second be used, and if there are duplicates in the second, will the third be used. (If no second or third are specified, Symphony will

simply arrange all the first sort key duplicates together without regard to any specific arrangement.)

Task — Re-sort
Command — FORM, MENU, SETTING, SORT KEYS
Command — FORM, MENU, NAME, CREATE
Explanation — There are two methods of re-sorting. The first is to go back to the settings sheet and change the sort keys. Simply follow the steps outlined above. The second is to create a new settings sheet, with different sort key settings. To accomplish this, backtrack a few paragraphs to where we created a new settings sheet for criterion, and follow the instructions.

Task — Remove underlining from form
Command — FORM, MENU, SETTINGS, UNDERSCORE
Explanation — This toggles the underlining mode back and forth between *off* and *on*.

Summary

In this chapter we've examined how we can manipulate a data base from a form window. In the next chapter we'll examine how we can manipulate directly from a SHEET environment.

CHAPTER
14

Integrating and
Printing Your
Data Base

Managing a data base from a SHEET environment is a more difficult task than from a FORM environment. It does, however, have certain advantages. From a sheet, we can work directly with the data base, instead of seeing it secondhand through forms. We can use special data functions with it. And, perhaps more importantly, we can integrate it with a spreadsheet we may have already created. We'll begin with this last important consideration — *integration*.

From Sheet Range To Data Base

In the last chapter you entered information into a data base by means of a form. This time we are going to do it differently. We are going to create a data base out of information which comes directly from our sheet. Let's assume you are working with a sales record, of which a small part appears below:

	A	B	C
	A	**B**	**C**
1	SALESPERSON	SALE	COMMISSION
2	Franks	325	32.5
3	Jones	100	10
4	Smith	1211	145.50
5	Franks	605	85
6	Miller	900	135
7	Smith	250	25

The above sheet entries are also suitable, *without modification*, to be used as our data base. Those readers who have not looked at the underlying sheet which Symphony created for us in the last few chapters may be surprised when I refer to the above illustration as a data base. It is, though. Each row represents a record, each column, a field. Instead of viewing them through an entry record, however, we are seeing them directly on the sheet.

This illustrates the power of Symphony. We can create a spreadsheet and then use it as a data base.

From the SHEET environment, all the data base controls are under the QUERY MENU. We reach this via SHEET, MENU, QUERY. The MENU headings are:

SETTINGS FIND EXTRACT UNIQUE DELETE RECORD-SORT PARSE QUIT

With these commands you can perform all of the functions available to you on the form window, and a few extra as well. In other words, you can manipulate the material you've created on your spreadsheet exactly as if it had been created specifically as a data base. Let's explore the various things you can do with this data base.

Select Records from the Data Base

Even though your sheet looks like a data base, it isn't yet set up for Symphony to treat it as such. First you have to tell SYMPHONY where it is and identify the ranges and fields.

Task — Identify the data base range for Symphony
Command — SHEET, MENU, QUERY, SETTINGS, BASIC, DATA BASE
Explanation — When you call up this command you are shown a settings sheet that is virtually identical to the form setting sheet (Figure 14.1).

If you were working from a FORM environment, and had used the GENERATE command, Symphony would have automatically defined a data base and a criterion range. However, since you are coming out of a SHEET environment, you must do this

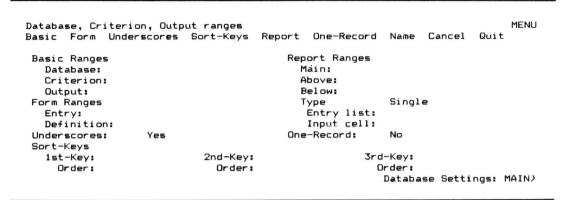

```
Database, Criterion, Output ranges                              MENU
Basic  Form  Underscores  Sort-Keys  Report  One-Record  Name  Cancel  Quit

Basic Ranges                            Report Ranges
  Database:                               Main:
  Criterion:                              Above:
  Output:                                 Below:
Form Ranges                               Type         Single
  Entry:                                    Entry list:
  Definition:                               Input cell:
Underscores:        Yes                 One-Record:      No
Sort-Keys
  1st-Key:                 2nd-Key:                 3rd-Key:
    Order:                   Order:                   Order:
                                             Database Settings: MAIN>
```

Fig. 14.1 Empty Settings Sheet.

yourself. The first step is to identify the data base range. Use the SETTINGS, BASIC, DATABASE command. Now indicate the *entire* range (in this case A1. . .C7). *Note*: you should indicate those cells which contain values and which you want Symphony to treat as labels. Otherwise, they will be handled as values.

Note also that if you want to *add* entries to the data base, you must do it before this point on the sheet. Then you must expand the data base range to accommodate the new entries.

Task — Identify a criteria range
Command — SHEET, MENU, QUERY, SETTINGS, BASIC, CRITERIA
Explanation — In order to select records out of the data base, you must have a way of telling Symphony what criteria you want it to use. In the FORM environment, Symphony automatically generated a criteria range for you. Here you must do it yourself. The criteria range need not be anything fancy. Any set of cells listing the titles of each field (column) will do. Here is a typical criteria range created on a sheet:

	A	B	C	
1	SALESPERSON	SALE	COMMISSION	
2	Franks	325	32.5	
3	Jones	100	10	
4	Smith	1211	145.50	
5	Franks	605	85	
6	Miller	900	135	
7	Smith	250	25	
8				
9				
10	SALESPERSON	SALE	COMMISSION	CRITERIA
11				RANGE
12				
13				
14				

The criteria range are the cells A10. .C11. The headings correspond to the column headings in the range you have defined as your data base. These are your fields (row 10). The next row (11) is the one in which you will enter criteria. Symphony will match the criteria from the fields in row 10 and 11, with the data in your data base (A1. .C7), and select what you want. After typing in the appropriate information, just indicate the cells with the pointer.

Task — Find matching records selected by criteria
Command — SHEET, MENU, QUERY, FIND
Explanation — Once you've established the data base and criteria range you can enter a criteria. Suppose you enter Smith in your criteria range.

Now you can ask Symphony to *find* each occurrence of "Smith." To do this use the commands indicated above. Symphony will start at the top of the data base and search through it, highlighting in turn each record in which Smith occurs. The [**UP ARROW**] and [**DOWN ARROW**] can be used to move up and down between occurrences.

Task — Create an output range
Command — SHEET, MENU, QUERY, BASIC, OUTPUT
Explanation — Perhaps rather than simply seeing the records *highlighted*, you'd like to see them *isolated*, much as we do when we examine records selected by criteria in the form window. When we were working in a FORM ENVIRONMENT, however, Symphony could display the selected records in the form window. Here, Symphony has no separate place to put the records selected out of the data base. Consequently, you have to create an *output range*. Symphony will dump all the records matched by criteria in this range.

The output range can be any convenient group of cells. So that Symphony can identify it, the range should contain the names of the fields in the data base. (It doesn't need to contain all the names, though.) For example, here's the sheet with an output range:

	A	B	C	
1	SALESPERSON	SALE	COMMISSION	
2	Franks	325	32.5	
3	Jones	100	10	
4	Smith	1211	145.50	
5	Franks	605	85	
6	Miller	900	135	
7	Smith	250	25	
8				
9				
10	SALESPERSON	SALE	COMMISSION	CRITERIA
11	Smith			RANGE
12				
13				
14				

	A	**B**	**C**
15	SALESPERSON	SALE	COMMISSION	OUTPUT
16				RANGE
17				
18				
19				
20				

When you execute the above command and Symphony asks for your output range, just specify cells A15. .C20. (Be sure the output range is large enough to accommodate all of the potential output you may have.)

Task — Output all records matching a criteria
Command — SHEET, MENU, QUERY, EXTRACT
Explanation — At this point you write what you want Symphony to find. Be sure that it is in the appropriate spot in the criteria range. For example, you would write in, Smith, under the Salesperson heading.

Now go to EXTRACT. Symphony will immediately search the data base and extract all records (rows) containing Smith and dump them in the output range. The range would look like this:

15	SALESPERSON	SALE	COMMISSION	OUTPUT
16	Smith	1211	145.50	RANGE
17	Smith	250	25	

Task — Select matching records, eliminating duplicates
Command — SHEET, MENU, QUERY, UNIQUE
Explanation — This command works just like EXTRACT, except that it eliminates duplicates.

Task — Delete records based on criteria
Command — SHEET, MENU, QUERY, DELETE
Explanation — Instead of just finding records according to specified criteria, this command will find them *and* delete them. *Warning*: Be careful with this command. Once deleted, the information is *gone for good!*

Task — Sort the data base
Command — SHEET, MENU, QUERY, RECORD-SORT
Explanation — The record-sort function works exactly as it does in the form window. See the explanation in the last chapter.

The PARSE Command

Task — Match input to fit the data base
Command — SHEET, MENU, QUERY, PARSE

Explanation — Thus far we have been talking about how to sort or select material and get it out of the data base. However, Symphony has an additional command that is very helpful in adding data to a data base.

The PARSE command breaks up data so that it will fit into the columns of a data base. For example, say you have a data base of three columns, each nine characters wide (due to the default setting; we could have made them any width). Perhaps we want to enter a long string of 25 characters from some other part of our worksheet. We now use the PARSE command. It will break up the long string so that the first nine characters will be in the first column, the second nine in the second column, and the remaining seven in the last column. *Note*: PARSE only works if you have a definition and a data base range defined—use the FORM, GENERATE command.

We can enhance the action of PARSE by specifying the *type* each column is to be. For example, if, as part of our data base, we define the Salesperson column to be a label only and the other two column/fields as values only, then PARSE will only enter a label in the first column, and values in the second. Thus, if in another cell in our worksheet we had written out, "Allen900", PARSE would put the label, Allen, in the first column, and the value, 900, in the second.

When we hit PARSE, we are first asked for the *parse range*. We name the cell(s) we want Symphony to "parcel" out. Next we are asked for a *review range*. This is where PARSE will dump any extraneous material. We can specify one or more cells here.

Be sure you have properly defined your data base, and your parse and review ranges, before engaging the PARSE command, otherwise the entire Symphony program could go on the blink. If this happens, you will have to reboot and start from scratch. You could lose anything you had not previously saved.

Data Base Statistical Functions

These are identical to the statistical functions discussed earlier under SHEET. For a complete explanation of each function, see Chapter 7.

They include:

@DSUM	@DMAX	@DSTD
@DAVG	@DMIN	@DVAR
@DCOUNT		

These functions operate on a selected field within the data base. To use them, select a cell adjacent to the data base, and enter the function in the following manner:

1. First write in the function — @SUM

2. Create an arugument, the first part of which is the data base range—(A1. .C7)

3. The second part of the argument is the column in the data base you want the function to operate on—,1,.

The last part of the argument specifies the criteria range ,A10. .C11). When you enter an item in the criteria range, the function will then operate on the field/column, and on those items within the field which are indicated in the criteria.

The form thus becomes:

@SUM(A1. .C7,1,A10. .A11)

Printing From Your Data Base

Printing from your data base can be as simple or as complex as you want it to be. It all depends on what you want to accomplish. In this chapter we are going to concentrate on simple tasks and only suggest some more sophisticated techniques.

There are essentially three major types of data base printing that most of us use. They are *reports, mailing labels* and *mailmerge* (merging of mailing labels with a form letter). We'll consider all three.

Printing the Report

In order to print a report, we need to have our data base set up. We'll assume you've created one through the form window. If that's the case, then printing it is just a matter of following these steps:

Task — Simple print-out of a data base
Command — FORM, SERVICES, PRINT, SETTINGS, SOURCE, DATABASE, GO
Explanation — Once you are in the form environment, simply issue the above commands. Symphony will obediently print out your data base. Notice that Symphony automatically prints out the field labels, as well as the records.

Task — Print in condensed type
Command — FORM, SERVICES, PRINT, INIT-STRING
Explanation — Some printers have a condensed type that reduces the spacing between letters. This type style is useful when you have a data base that is larger than the width of your paper.

If your printer has such a capability you can usually access it by sending to the printer the initialization string, which sets it up for condensed print. To do this you must use DECIMAL in the form of three numbers following a slash. For example, \ 018 would set up condensed print on most Epson printers. Check your printer manual for the appropriate code.

Additionally, you can adjust the width of the columns or the margins you are using (from the PRINT MENU) to accommodate a difficult printing task.

Task — Add an identification line
Command — FORM, MENU, SETTINGS, REPORT, BELOW
Explanation — You can add a comment at the bottom of your report, such as, "Mailing addresses for the F-212 Report." To do this simply type the line in a convenient cell. It will be printed at the bottom of the report. Then execute the above command. When you get to BELOW, you will be asked for the range. Simply fill in the cell in which you wrote your comment; it will print out as indicated. *Note:* you can also incorporate a formula here with any of the statistical functions discussed in the last chapter. These can also be placed on the *ABOVE report range.*

Task — Print only a portion of the data base
Command — DATA BASE RANGE
Explanation — On the form, settings sheet, specify a range smaller than the full data base range. Whatever you specify will be printed.

Task — Print only selected records
Command — CRITERIA RANGE
Explanation — We saw earlier that if you call up the form, settings sheet, it has a data base and a criteria range in the upper left hand corner. For the print-out indicated above, we assumed that the data base range was filled (by Symphony, when we used GENERATE to create our forms), while the criteria range was left empty. If you insert criteria in this range, then Symphony will only print out according to the criteria selected.

Task — Print in the form of labels
Explanation — The print commands are essentially the same. What you need to do, however, is to tell Symphony that instead of printing each record in the mailing list data base horizontally, it should print it vertically.

   This requires setting up a different format for the report range on the form, settings sheet. It's quite simple. To create a vertical format, simply select a range of convenient vertical cells in your sheet. Then enter what you want to be printed out in the vertical range. There are several ways of doing this, but I've found the following to be the easiest:

```
COLUMN OF CELLS
    +A50 (Refers to the first NAME cell in our data base)
    +B50 (Refers to the first ADDRESS cell in our data base)    FORM
    +C50 (Refers to the first CITY & STATE cell)                SETTINGS
    +D50 (Refers to the first ZIP code cell)                    REPORT
    BLANK                                                        MAIN
    BLANK
```

   In the first cell of the vertical range, you put the cell location of the first *name* that appears in your data base. In the next cell, you put the cell location of the first *address* from your data base. In the next cell you put the cell location of the first *city* and *state*. In the next goes the *zip code*. Now, place these cells in FORM, SETTINGS, REPORT, MAIN.

Be sure to leave as many blank cells as you want lines to be left out between the labels. (This is for proper placement. Some trial and error may be needed here.) Notice that the "+" sign is used to indicate that you have entered formulas in the cells in this range.

Before you print, you need to check the *form, menu, settings* sheet to be sure that the ABOVE and BELOW report ranges are empty (otherwise you will print a header and a footer). If they are filled, empty them (using the CANCEL command will empty the entire report range.

Then follow the procedure described previously for printing a report. The print-out should look like this:

```
- - - - - - - -

Pete Smith
23 Elm St.
Falls Church, VA
22043


- - - - - - - -

Gladys Miller
12 Empire Dr.
New York, NY
10021


- - - - - - - -

Paul Jones
14 Maple Rd.
Costa Mesa, CA
92626


- - - - - - - -
```

Fig. 14.2 Address Label Print-Out.

Note: Be sure your roll of address labels is properly inserted in your printer before printing.

Task — Make multiple passes
Command — FORM, MENU, SETTINGS, REPORT, TYPE, MULTIPLE
Explanation — Using the TYPE, MULTIPLE command, you can ask Symphony to make multiple passes through the data base, producing reports from selected fields on the basis of each pass. This can be particularly helpful if the data base includes zip codes.

Task — Merge mailing labels with a form letter

Explanation — Often we will want to create a form letter which we can merge with a mailing label data base. This means that as Symphony types the letter, it will automatically insert a different name or other data in each copy.

The overall procedure is quite simple and follows the example described above for the mailing label list. The only difference is that you are telling Symphony to print a letter around each label.

To begin, create your letter in a DOC environment. Where you are going to substitute from the data base, use a field name. Here's what the letter might look like:

December 5, 1985

NAME
ADDRESS
CITY, STATE, & ZIP

Dear NAME:

Just a quick note to let you know we've changed our address. We are now located at:

    Tower Corporation
    2345 Smith St.
    Los Angeles, Calif.

We look forward to welcoming you soon to our new offices.

You are going to fill in all the field names with data from records, so be sure you leave yourself enough room to write in the specific names and addresses. (This is particularly important if you're entering material in the middle of a sentence.)

You'll recall that all entries in a DOC environment are entered in the cells in column A. However, when we enter records from our data base, they come not from a DOC, but a SHEET environment. Thus they will go in the cells in whatever column is on the underlying sheet. A mismatch of locations could occur. To avoid this, you must now switch to a sheet window, and enter the record cells there.

Wherever there is a generic entry, substitute the formula for your fields, just as you did with labels. The letter should now look like this:

December 5, 1985

+A50
+B50
+C50&" "&D50

Dear +A50:

Just a quick note to let you know we've changed our address. We are now located at:

> Tower Corporation
> 2345 Smith St Los Angeles, Calif.

We look forward to welcoming you soon to our new offices.
: :

In this letter we have combined the field for City and State on the same line with the field for Zip. We could also have had separate fields for first and last name, as well as fields for other information. Using the &, you can connect these fields at any particular location (see the chapters on SHEET). You'll notice also that there is a *page break* (: :) at the end of the letter. This ensures that each letter will print on a separate page.

In order to print, we must now tell Symphony where the report is. You would move to a FORM environment and call up the settings sheet. Then, in the MAIN report range, you would indicate the full range of the letter. The letter now becomes your report.

Then you would just print out in the normal fashion. You would get as many letters as there are reports in your data base.

```
December 5, 1985


Paul Jones
14 Maple St.
Costa Mesa, CA

Dear Paul:

Just a quick note to let you know we've changed our address.
We are now located at:
          Tower Corporation
          2345 Smith St.
          Los Angeles, Calif.
We look forward to welcoming you soon to our new office.
```

Fig. 14.3 Print-Out of Finished Letter.

CHAPTER
15

Communications

Symphony includes a special communications program that allows you to send and receive files and messages between your computer and another. The program is fairly simple to operate. However, communications in general tends to be a sophisticated and complex field.

In this chapter we are going to explore how to use the Symphony communications program. Along the way I'll suggest the most common settings. It is beyond the scope of this book, however, to give detailed explanations of communications theory or terminology. For those interested in a deeper examination of communications, you can find many excellent books available on the subject in leading bookstores.

Before getting started, it is important to understand that communications with Symphony requires a *modem*. With a modem, the signal that a computer generates can be changed so that it can be interpreted through telephone lines. Then the modem changes the signal back again. You must have a modem in order to use Symphony's communication program. (Some computers come with built-in modems. Others require a separate external modem. Check with your computer's manual.)

Also, to use the communications program you must select the modem and the *communications port* during the Symphony INSTALL program.

There are essentially two parts to computer communications. The first is called the "set up." This means that sending and receiving computers are programmed so that they can communicate with each other. The second part is the actual transmission of files or other information.

We'll begin with the set up (which many computer users consider to be the most critical factor). Later in the chapter we'll explore the ways to send and transmit data.

Set Up

Those new to communications frequently ask, "Why is it necessary to set up? Why not simply connect the computers and be done with it?" The reason is that there are many ways of configuring the computer to send and receive a signal. Unless both computers are configured identically, they won't understand each other. It's similar to two people, one French, the other, English, trying to converse over a phone line. There may be some conversation, but most of it will be lost because of the lack of a common language.

Settings

The most vital part of setting up, therefore, is establishing the *communications parameters*. We begin by calling up the COMMUNICATIONS environment using the ALT and MENU keys ([**ALT**] plus [**F10**]). This puts us in a *comm window*. Now we hit MENU, SETTINGS. This brings up the communications settings sheet (Figure 15.1).

```
Speed and type of transmission                                      MENU
Interface  Phone  Terminal  Send  Break  Handshaking  Capture  Login  Name  Quit

  Interface            Terminal                 Send
    Baud:      110        Screen:    Window        EOL:       \m
    Parity:    None       Echo:      No            Delay:     0
    Length:    7          Linefeed:  No            Response:  \j
    Stop bits: 1          Backspace: Backspace   Break:       60
  Phone                   Wrap:      Yes         Handshaking
    Type:      Pulse      Delay:     0             Inbound:   Yes
    Dial:      60         Translation:            Outbound:  Yes
    Answer:    15           (none)              Capture:
    Number:                                       Range:     No
                                                  Printer:   No
                                        -Communications Settings:

15-Jan-85  01:42 AM
```

Fig. 15.1 COMM Settings Sheet.

This sheet displays all the parameters of our computer's communications settings. In order to communicate, we must set our computer to the exact *same* settings as those of the computer we plan to "talk" to.

How do we know what the other computer's settings are? Usually the computer that does the calling must match the computer that receives the call. If you are doing the sending, you will need to check with the user of the receiving computer, to find out the proper parameters. Once you know what the parameters are, you can set your computer accordingly, using the SETTINGS MENU. The SETTINGS MENU contains both vital and incidental material. Most of the vital material is under the INTERFACE heading. Chances are that 90 percent of the time the only area of settings you will be concerned with will be INTERFACE.

We'll cover INTERFACE here, and for convenience, we will also cover most of the remainder of the information you need to know concerning SETTINGS, many of which are not as important.

Interface

We'll take these important settings one at a time:

Baud — This is the *speed* at which the signal is communicated. We are given a selection of eight numbers, each of which corresponds to a different baud rate. (Check the settings sheet as you select a number, and watch the rate change.) The most common transmissions today are "slow," which is number 3 (300 baud) and "fast" which is number 5 (1200 baud). "Very slow," or number 1 (110 baud), is also used occasionally.

Parity — This refers to error checking of the signal. There are three possible settings. They correspond to the following:

3   = Even
2   = Odd
1   = None

Length — This refers to whether the full eight bit byte is sent, or whether only seven bits are sent. (*Bits* are discrete units of information.) We are given two settings:

2   = Eight bits
1   = Seven bits

Stop Bits — This refers to the number of bits inserted *after* a character, so that the receiving computer will be able to distinguish that character. Our choices are:

2   = Two stop bits
1   = One stop bit

Most transmissions will use one stop bit.

Phone

These settings refer to the type of phone being used. The command has four subheadings, which are briefly explained.

Type — There are either touch (tone) or rotary (pulse).

Dial-Time — Refers to how much time you allow for the call to be completed. (60 to 120 seconds is common.)

Answer-Time — How much time should be allotted to making a connection after the other side picks up the phone. (15 to 60 seconds is typical.)

Number — This is a default phone number that you enter. If at the time of establishing communications, you don't enter a different number, Symphony will dial this number. Type it the way you would a regular phone number, with dashes. Symphony will ignore these and just pay attention to the numbers.

Terminal

This allows you to set up your *comm window*. It should work without your having to use these commands, however, we'll cover them briefly should you have any need for them:

Screen — You have a choice between using a window or the full screen. The full-screen option may be useful when receiving from a computer that sends data in a large format.

Echo — This can determine whether or not the message you are sending also appears on your screen. A "yes" generates a screen echo from your computer. A "no" will require an echo to come from the receiving computer (otherwise your screen will remain blank). *Echo* simply means that you are able to see on your screen the data that is being transmitted.

Linefeed — The best way to handle this command is to look at the transmission being received. If each new line overlays the previous line, destroying it, then you need this command in "yes" position.

Backspace — This configures the [**BACKSPACE**]. Selecting *Backspace* will allow the [**BACKSPACE**] to act like the [**LEFT ARROW**]. Selecting *delete* will allow the [**BACKSPACE**] to act like the [**RIGHT ARROW**] deleting as it goes.

Wrap — This allows lines longer than the window to wrap around so that you can see them. The usual setting is "yes."

Delay — This delays the transmission (so the other computer can catch up). It's usually better to use a slower baud rate than to use *delay*.

Translation — Sometimes different computers generate different symbols for codes used between them. (This allows you to use standard or customized translation tables.) Translation is a technical subject and requires an advanced understanding of computer codes and transmission. Check with a book that specializes in communications.

Send

These controls are useful when you are transmitting a sheet file. They are used with the TRANSMIT-RANGE command, and will be covered in the next section on sending and receiving data.

Break

This sends a signal to the receiving computer to break off receiving and come back on line. The duration in milliseconds can be set with this command.

Handshaking

Handshaking refers to the balancing of transmission so that the sending machine doesn't send more than the receiving machine can handle. The selections are inbound/ outbound and yes/no for each.

With both settings *on*, the protocol (a mutually agreed upon procedure for communicating) is X-On/X-Off. This usually sees the most use. You can customize it by turning either, or both, inbound/outbound *off*.

Capture

These controls are used when you are receiving a spreadsheet. We'll go over them in the next section.

≡Sending and Receiving

Now that we've established the basic parameters, we'll go on to take a look at how you would actually phone another computer and send and receive data.

Sending

Task — Phone another computer
Command — COMMUNICATIONS, MENU, PHONE, CALL
Explanation — When you call up this command, Symphony will ask what phone number you want to call. Just type in the number. Symphony will display the message, "Dialing" and you will be asked to wait while it tries to establish communications. This amount of time Symphony uses to establish communications depends on what you entered on the Dial-Time on your settings sheet. (The default was 60 seconds.)

Once communications are established, your modem may signal with a *tone*. Typically, you should now hit [ENTER] several times, to let the other computer know you are on line. (Some computers require a special key to establish communications — be sure you're aware of this before connecting.)

If Symphony is unable to establish communications it will break off and signal ERROR on the upper right hand corner of the screen. You can now try again.

Task — Answer an incoming call

Command — COMMUNICATIONS, MENU, PHONE, WAIT-MODE
Command — COMMUNICATIONS, MENU, PHONE, ANSWER
Explanation — Symphony offers two options here. The WAIT-MODE command instructs your modem to wait for an incoming call and then to answer it. Your modem must have the ability to do this, in order to use this command.

The ANSWER command allows you to answer a call yourself. Typically, an external modem will signal an incoming call with a ringing sound. If you call up the comm window you will see RING displayed on the screen. Just hit the ANSWER command and Symphony will attempt to answer the call. It will display the message, ANSWER-ING.

If the connection is made, Symphony will respond by displaying ONLINE. If no connection is made, an ERROR message may flash, or a NO CARRIER message may occur.

Task — "Talk" to another computer
Command — WRITE
Explanation — Once communications are established you can begin to write in your comm window. The information will also appear on the screen of the other computer. Similarly, what that user types in should appear on your screen.

Trouble-Shooting

The most common problem in communications is using the wrong baud rate (the wrong speed of transmission). Typically this shows up as unintelligible letters and numbers on the screen. Go back and check your SETTINGS, BAUD rate. Be sure it's the same as the computer you are attempting to communicate with.

If your *echo* is *off*, and the other computer isn't sending an echo, your screen may be blank. Check the SETTINGS, ECHO to see that it's turned *on*. If there is a double image on the screen, check the SETTINGS, ECHO to see that it is *off*.

If you still have problems, be sure that your WORD LENGTH is set the same as the other computer's, and that your modem is properly connected.

When you have persistent problems don't overlook the possibility that the other computer isn't set up to the parameters that its user gave you. Establishing communications protocol is tricky, particularly for first-time users. Trial and error, however, usually solves most problems.

Task — Hang up
Command — COMMUNICATIONS, MENU, PHONE, HANGUP
Explanation — You want to break the connection. Just use this command.

Task — Talk over the phone line that the computer is using
Command — COMMUNICATIONS, MENU, PHONE, VOICE-MODE/DATA-MODE
Explanation — If your modem has the proper features, then you can switch between *computer communications* and *voice communications* using this command.

Task — Log in to another computer
Command — COMMUNICATIONS, MENU, LOGIN
Explanation — In order to access some computers, particularly main frames computers, you may be required to supply a series of special codes. This command automatically feeds the codes to the receiving computer. (You must, of course, know what these codes are before you send them.) Similarly, Symphony can require a sending computer to log in with predetermined codes, before it will allow a message to be received.

Before using LOGIN, you must tell Symphony what the codes are, and how you want them sent (received). You establish these parameters through COMMUNICATIONS, MENU, SETTINGS, LOGIN command. There you will see the following menu:

MAXIMUM-TIME   REPEAT-TIME A B C D E F G H I J NEW QUIT

The commands are self-explanatory. *Maximum* and *repeat time* determine how long Symphony has to feed/receive the codes, and how many times to repeat the sequence if the information fails to get through the first time. The letters indicate where you log in the codes. (Start with A for the first code. If there's a second sequence, then go to B, and so forth.) NEW erases all the settings so that you start off with a clean slate.

Task — Send or receive a file
Command — COMMUNICATIONS, MENU, FILE-TRANSFER
Explanation — This command allows us to send or receive files to or from a disk. It is really quite simple, although time consuming (depending on the baud rate of our transmission).

When we invoke this command, we are first asked whether we want to send or receive. If we want to send, we are asked to name the file in the active drive. This is done with the pointer, in the normal fashion. If we want to receive, we are similarly asked to name a file to receive the data.

Once the file has been named, Symphony begins transmission. Two messages may occur. The first is, "WAITING FOR CONNECTION". This indicates that the receiving computer is not yet ready to receive the file.

"?BYTES OUT OF ? BYTES SENT - ? ERRORS CORRECTED tells us how many bytes are in a file and how many have been sent. The last question mark represents the number of times blocks of bytes had to be re-sent because errors occurred.

Note: in both sending and receiving activities the files go from disk to disk. We have to wait for transmission to end before we can call up the file from the disk to work on it.

Task — Send all, or part of an active sheet (range)
Command — COMMUNICATIONS, MENU, TRANSMIT-RANGE
Explanation — We can transmit any range on our SHEET with this command. It asks us for the range, we specify it in the usual manner, and Symphony then sends it. *Note*: Symphony does not send the SHEET format, only the data within it. The result is that

what is sent amounts to a series of data entries. For example, suppose we wanted to transmit the following data from our worksheet:

	A	B	C	D
1	NUTS	BOLTS	SCREWS	HAMMERS
2	437	437		12

Using the TRANSMIT-RANGE command, we can send this information directly. It will look like this, however:

```
NUTS  BOLTS  SCREWS  HAMMERS
437   437   12
```

You probably noticed that the column divisions are no longer there. Rather, the data is transmitted as a *row*. Empty columns have been ignored. A receiving computer must be able to handle this type of transmission and convert it to useful data. To avoid this problem use the FILE-TRANSFER command.

Receiving

Task — Help the receiving computer to receive a range
Command — COMMUNICATIONS, MENU, SETTINGS, SEND
Explanation — There are several settings under this command which can be useful, particularly in allowing the receiving computer to pick up our transmission correctly. These settings are set up *prior* to sending a range:

EOL (end of line) — We can insert a linefeed, plus additional commands with this command. The default is \ 013 (decimal) or \ M. which sends a carriage return. A linefeed is decimal \ 010 or \ J. The ESCAPE command is decimal \ 027. (Don't forget the slash mark before the code.)

Delay — This instructs Symphony to delay the time between the sending of lines. You set the specified wait-time in increments of 1/128th of a second. For normal transmission, the default is set at zero. For a range transmission, however, you may want to set a delay time.

Response — Symphony must receive this code before sending the next line of data. The default is set to \ j. You can, however, change to another code, depending on the sending computer's parameters.

Task — Capture a transmission directly to the spreadsheet
Command — COMMUNICATIONS, SETTINGS, CAPTURE
Explanation — This settings command allows you to specify a range where you want data to be sent directly to your active spreadsheet.

To activate this command, simply indicate a range of your sheet where you want the captured data to go. You should specify an empty, and out-of-the way location.

The actual "capturing" mode can be turned on by using CAPTURE ([**F4**]). It can be cancelled or erased, using the commands for CAPTURE in the COMMUNICATIONS, SETTINGS sheet.

Task — Capture a transmission directly to the printer
Command — COMMUNICATIONS, SETTINGS, CAPTURE, PRINTER
Explanation — Follow the instructions above, but have the data sent to the *printer*, instead of the sheet.

Task — Capture a document directly to the spreadsheet
Command — SHEET, MENU, WIDTH
Explanation — A document, under the Symphony program, is actually a long label entirely held in the A column. To capture a document to an active sheet, therefore, it is necessary to do two steps. First, indicate the capture range to be column A only. (Be sure the range is very long, to accommodate the entire document.) Second, expand the width of column A on your sheet to accommodate the width of the incoming data. Remember, the width of a column can be expanded up to 240 characters. Typically, 80 will do.

The document will be captured, with each line appearing in a separate cell in column A. This can then be easily transferred to a DOCUMENT environment for editing.

Macro Programs

One of Symphony's advanced features is its ability to let us create our own programs directly within it. Although I refer to this as an "advanced" feature, it is not difficult, even for beginners. We'll consider it here, you will undoubtedly find it very useful.

At a higher level of advanced programming, however, Symphony's macros defined below, and the Symphony programming language, are quite sophisticated and well beyond the range of this book. I suggest that if you would like to explore this further, you consult books on programming which deal specifically with this topic.

Why Should We Program?

The best answer is to study an example. Let's say you are using Symphony's SHEET environment for a business application, and you find that you are repeatedly using the following labels to head up different parts of your SHEET:

	A	B	C	D	E
1	SALESPERSON	Sales	Commission	Commission	Total
2		Itemized	Rate	Amount	Income
3	Sally				
4	James				
5	Henry				
6	Harold				

To write them out over and over again is very tedious. Of course, there are alternate methods. You could keep them on a separate file and call them up when you needed them. But, again, that is tedious.

A macro, however, could solve the problem. With a macro, you could program Symphony to call up the labels whenever you needed them. All you would need to do is type in a name you assign to them. Let's say you called them, Labels. To access the above display, all you would need to do, then, is type in one command key, the word Labels, hit [**ENTER**], and the entire set of labels would be typed onto your screen by Symphony automatically. With a macro, then, you can teach Symphony to write out data and commands. Then Symphony will present them any way that you want. However, we've only scratched the surface. We'll see even more benefits of macros as we learn to use one.

Creating a Macro

The essence of a macro is that it repeats a series of commands and keystrokes that we create.

Task — Create a macro
Explanation — There are several steps and several commands involved. We'll go through them one by one.

LEARN — You have to turn Symphony's *learn mode* on, so that it will know you want it to learn what you are teaching. Turn on LEARN by calling up SERVICES, SETTINGS, LEARN. This in turn produces another menu. Most of the terms on it are self-explanatory (assuming you've already read through this book). You will be using the first command, RANGE.

Symphony is asking where you want to place the range of cells that it will use to learn your macro program (you must pick a single column). Pick a range that is out of the way of your data, yet large enough to encompass all the commands and strokes you may want to use. (You don't want to go all the way to the far end of the SHEET, though, as that will use up too much memory). I suggest picking a *column* to the right of your work. In this case, pick column "X".

You'll also need to make sure the range itself is sufficiently long to accommodate all your typing strokes. In this case, go from X1 to X200, or 200 rows. Use the pointer to indicate your range as X1. .X200.

NAMING — Once you have your learning range, you now must give it a name. (All macros must be named.) Use the standard method of naming a range — MENU, RANGE, NAME, CREATE. *Be sure the name you assign goes into the first (top) cell of the macro learn range.* In this case, the macro, LABEL. You can also use a double stroke, such as \ A to name a label. You would then call it up using [**ALT**] plus [**A**].

PROGRAMMING — Now you're ready to "teach" Symphony. Go to some *unused* portion of the SHEET. Hit the [**LEARN**] or [**ALT**] plus [**F5**], and type in your labels *exactly* as you want them to appear.

As you do this, two things happen. You see the labels on the screen as you type them. Also, in your learn range (which you can view if your typing cells happen to be close by), Symphony enters not only the labels themselves, but all the keystrokes required to create them, as well. Here's what Symphony enters as you type in the chart:

LABELS (name)

SALESPERSON{RIGHT}
Sales{RIGHT}
Commission{RIGHT}
Commission{RIGHT}
Total{DOWN}
Income{LEFT}
Amount{LEFT}
Rate{LEFT}
Itemized{LEFT}
{DOWN}
Sally{DOWN}
James{DOWN}
Henry{DOWN}
Harold∿

Note: Symphony types in *all* your keystrokes, including mistakes.

When you've finished teaching Symphony, your macro (that is, finished typing in the labels for your chart), hit [**LEARN**] or [**ALT**] plus [**F5**] again, and turn LEARN *off*. Now go back, using the editing functions (erase, move, copy), to correct any errors you may have made in the learn range. (*Don't leave any empty cells* in the learn range. Symphony will begin the macro and continue only until it hits an empty cell. Then it will stop.)

⊞sing Macros

Task — Use a macro
Command — USER KEY [**F7**] plus MACRO NAME
Explanation — Using a macro is easy. Just aim the pointer where you want the results to appear. (They will appear below and to the right of the pointer.) Hit [**USER**] [**F7**], and type in the *exact* name of the macro. Symphony will do the rest. The items you originally programmed in during the LEARN mode should be retyped out, in exactly the same order. In this case, your chart of labels should appear.

You probably noticed that Symphony repeats exactly what you originally typed, which includes more than just labels. It includes directions and commands, as well.

(The only keys Symphony cannot learn are [**NUM LOCK**] and [**SCROLL LOCK**].) Thus, you can expand your horizons and use the macros for an enormous range of uses. In addition, there are also many functions commands that can be used with macros.

Additionally, there may be times when you want a macro to start as soon as you turn on Symphony. This can be done using AUTO-EXECUTE.

Task — Start a macro when Symphony is turned on
Command — SERVICES, SETTINGS, AUTO-EXECUTE
Explanation — Your macro must have been created previously for this to work. When you call up this command, just aim the pointer at the cell containing your macro's name (or write in the name itself). When Symphony starts, it will automatically call up the macro that you want.

CHAPTER 17

File Management, Printing and Other Services

≣ile Management

File management simply means the ability to save, retrieve and work with files we've created. Symphony provides a quick and easy method of accomplishing this. It's best to study Symphony's file management system, particularly the methods of saving and retrieval, before going on to do any extensive work in the program.

The items involved in file management are:

NAMING

SAVING

RETRIEVING

ERASING

We'll explore each of these, along with their variations.

Symphony's file management system is located through the SERVICES, FILE MENU shown below:

SAVE RETRIEVE COMBINE EXTRACT ERASE BYTES LIST
TABLE IMPORT DIR

Task — Write a file name

Command — EIGHT CHARACTERS

Explanation — Symphony's system for naming files is essentially the same as the MS DOS operating system. This means you can use any eight characters, including letters of the alphabet, numbers, dollar and percent signs, and a few other symbols. (Excluded are " : ; * ∿ . , and several others; check your DOS manual.)

Under the file name system, you can put a period at the end of a name and add a three character suffix. However, it is not advisable to do this because Symphony automatically adds its own suffix. Symphony will not display files which do not have a suffix it can use. In most cases this is the suffix .WRK (work), which it puts on the data files that you have created. Here are the suffixes Symphony works with:

.WRK — WORK
.PIC — GRAPH FILE (Use to create a graphic "picture")
.CNF — CONFIGURATION (Configures Symphony)
.PRN — PRINT (Printing to disk instead of printer)
.CTF — CHARACTER TRANSLATION FILE (Used in communications)

Saving

Task — Save a file

Command — SERVICES, FILE, SAVE

Explanation — Symphony "writes" whatever you have created into your computer's temporary RAM memory. To save the information permanently, you must store it on the disk.

If you have never saved or retrieved the current file, then when you call up SAVE, Symphony displays the command, plus its guess for the disk. Usually this is disk A: \ . For example:

Save file name: A: \

Symphony uses the entire name for a disk such as A: \ , B: \ or C: \ . (Don't forget the slash symbol.)

Then you simply type in a name and hit **[ENTER]**. Symphony will save the file on the A disk.

On the other hand, if you want to save your file on a different disk, you can hit **[ESC]** (to remove the current disk drive name). Then type in a new drive and name, such as:

B: \ LETTER

Symphony will now save the file to a disk in the B drive. (See the explanation on DIRECTORY, for changing the default drive.)

Previously Saved File

If you have previously saved or retrieved a file, when you call up SAVE, Symphony will display the file name as:

Save file name: A: \ LETTER

To save on disk A, merely hit **[ENTER]**. Symphony will ask:

File with that name already exists — Replace it? (YES/NO).

If you answer YES, the original file will be destroyed and then replaced with the current file. This is useful if you are saving every screenful or so of material as you are working along, and want to continuously update your save. If you answer NO, the old file will remain. You then have the option of giving the current file a new name. *Note*: see the chapters on graphs for special instructions on saving a graph file.

Task — Save only a part of the current sheet
Command — SERVICES, FILE, XTRACT
Explanation — This command allows you to save only a portion of a sheet. It is useful when you have a table or small section of work that you want stored so that you can retrieve it later, or retrieve repeatedly.

When you issue the command, you are asked, "Formulas/Values." If you select Formulas, Symphony will save the sheet exactly as it is, with labels, numbers and formulas. If you select Values, it will convert all formulas to numbers during the save process. After specifying "Formulas/Values," you need to indicate the range to be saved, and a file name.

Retrieval

Task — Retrieve a file
Command — SERVICES, FILE, RETRIEVE
Explanation — This is somewhat tricky, and can result in the erasure of valuable material if you are not careful.

The RETRIEVE command searches your disk and calls up a directory. Then, just point to the file you want. It will appear on the screen.

The danger is that when you use RETRIEVE to obtain a file, you *automatically erase whatever file you were currently working on*. Furthermore, Symphony does not warn you about this.

Let's go through the process step-by-step. Execute the command. The menu line now lists, in alphabetical order, all files in the current disk drive. (You can ask for all the files in another drive by using [ESC] to clear the enter line, and then typing in another drive name, such as B: \ .)

If there are more files than can be displayed on the menu line, they can be viewed by hitting either [F9] or [F10]. A directory of files that you can access will appear on the screen.

Now use the arrow keys to point to the file you want retrieved. Then hit [ENTER]. Symphony will retrieve the file and *replace* whatever you have on the screen with the new file.

However, if you have important material on your screen, it is vital that you *first save* what you were working on *before* using RETRIEVE. Otherwise, it will be erased.

Task — Retrieve and combine sheet files
Command — SERVICES, FILE, COMBINE
Explanation — This command allows you to combine an existing file with a file that has been retrieved. (Remember, the RETRIEVE command results in erasing an existing file.)

To use this command, first place the cursor where you want the file that has been retrieved to go. It will be placed to the right and below the cursor. *Note*: BE CAREFUL! If you use COMBINE incorrectly you could lose valuable data.

When you invoke this command, you are given three options:

COPY   ADD   SUBTRACT

COPY means that the file that you retrieve will replace any data in the cells onto which it is copied. You are also asked if you want to copy "Values/Formulas." This simply means you can copy either the formulas, or the current values that the formulas represent.

ADD means that values in the file that you retrieve will be added to any values in the file in which you are working.

SUBTRACT means that values in the file that you are retrieving will be subtracted from any values in the current sheet.

In addition, Symphony asks whether you want the *entire* file to be retrieved, or only *a named portion* of it. To activate "Named Area," a specific area in the file must have been already named. (See naming ranges.)

Next, you are asked to "Ignore Read." This concerns conflicting range names between the two files. "Ignore" combines any duplicated names. "Read" will include the names.

Task — Change the default drive for *SAVE* or *RETRIEVE*
Command — SERVICES, FILE, DIRECTORY
Explanation — With either SAVE, or RETRIEVE, Symphony will guess A as the drive you want. What if you want B? The default can be changed to B with this command. Then, whenever you use SAVE or RETRIEVE, Symphony will assume you mean B drive.

Note: this change is temporary and lasts only as long as your current work session with Symphony. You can make the change permanent, however, by using the configuration commands, explained later in this chapter.

Task — Erase a file
Command — SERVICES, FILE, ERASE
Explanation — This command allows you to erase unwanted files. When you invoke it, you are shown another menu:

WORKSHEET   PRINT   GRAPH   OTHER

Each word describes a directory. If you choose WORKSHEET, you'll be shown a directory of all files with a .WRK suffix. PRINT takes you to .PRN suffixes and GRAPH to .PIC. To see all the files on the diskette, you could choose OTHER.

Once you see the files, use the pointer to indicate the one to be erased. Hitting [ENTER] erases the file.

Warning: Once you erase a file, it's gone forever.

These, then, are the basic file management commands. There are, however, several other commands which you can use. We'll cover each individually.

Other Commands

Task — Find out how much space is left on a disk
Command — SERVICES, FILE, BYTES
Explanation — This reads the disk and tells you how much usable space is left.

Task — Find out how much memory is left in RAM
Command — SERVICES, SETTINGS
Explanation — The first entry on the settings sheet expresses, in percentages, the amount of temporary RAM memory that has been used, and the amount that is left. The amount that is left will depend on the size of the RAM memory in your computer.

Task — Call up a directory on a disk
Command — SERVICES, FILE, LIST
Explanation — This command calls up a directory of the active disk. You have your choice of displaying files by four headings:

WORKSHEET   PRINT   GRAPH   ALL

You will see a directory of files according to the suffix you have selected.

Task — Create a table of files on the screen
Command — SERVICES, FILE, TABLE
Explanation — This writes onto your screen a table of the files that are in a disk. Be sure you place the cursor (pointer) at an *empty area*, before invoking this command. If you don't, it will overwrite whatever is written on your sheet or document.

Once you specify the disk drive, and the kind of file you want (WORKSHEET, PRINT, GRAPH, ALL), Symphony produces a table of the files on the screen. You can then save the table, and print it out if you wish.

Task — Retrieve a foreign file
Command — SERVICES, FILE, IMPORT
Explanation — This gives you a limited ability to read files that were not created by Symphony. When you invoke this command, you are given two options: TEXT and STRUCTURED.

TEXT can be useful to read a document created by a different word processing program. It than transforms that document into a sheet. (The foreign files must be standard ASCII files; that is, each line of the foreign document is written into a separate cell in the A column of the Symphony sheet. Since a cell has a limitation of 240 characters, longer lines may be partially lost.)

The STRUCTURED option is useful for reading foreign files which have numbers. The numbers will be inserted into cells in a Symphony sheet. Any labels enclosed by parentheses will also be inserted.

Note: this command causes Symphony to overwrite any existing material in the sheet (it's similar to RETRIEVE). Be sure you've selected an empty part of the sheet with your cursor before beginning.

File Errors

There are several errors which can occur when you are dealing with files. We will look at the two most common.

DISK FULL — You have tried to save a file, and this error appears. It means that the file was not saved, because you did not have enough memory space on the diskette. *Don't turn off your machine, or use* RETRIEVE, *or any other command that will cause the current file to be lost!*

With DISK-FULL, you have several options. You can insert another diskette with more room (it must have been previously formatted). You can erase some files from the current diskette, or you can transfer files from the current diskette to another. Then try to save the file again.

MEMORY FULL — This means that you have exhausted the computer's RAM memory. If you are operating with only the minimum amount of memory (320K), this may crop up often, particularly when you try to load a big spreadsheet.

Symphony will do the best it can to try to load as much of the spreadsheet as your computer's memory will allow. The best solution, however, is to have more memory installed in your computer.

Printing

In many cases, printing with Symphony simply means calling up the PRINT command and selecting the GO option. To stop the printer while it is operating, just hit [CONTROL] plus [BREAK]. Printing is covered in different sections of this book as it relates to specific applications. Here, however, let's look at the print commands in general.

When you call up the PRINT command, you are given this menu:

GO   LINE ADVANCE   PAGE ADVANCE   ALIGN   SETTINGS   QUIT

GO — Starts the printer.

[CONTROL] plus [BREAK] — Stops the printer.

LINE ADVANCE — Advances the paper one *line*.

PAGE ADVANCE — Advances the paper one *page*.

ALIGN — Resets Symphony's print facility so that it treats the printer as if it is at the start of a document. (Without this instruction, Symphony will begin printing again from the point it left off.) Use ALIGN every time you reset your printer.

SETTINGS — You use this sheet to tell Symphony how you want the printed page to look. We'll cover this in detail below. An example of the Print Settings Sheet is shown in Figure 17.1.

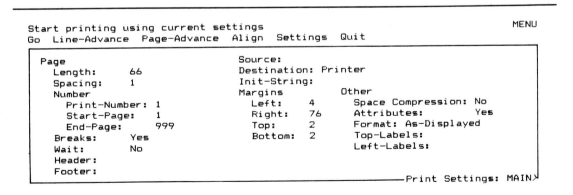

```
Start printing using current settings                          MENU
Go  Line-Advance  Page-Advance  Align  Settings  Quit

  Page                      Source:
    Length:      66         Destination: Printer
    Spacing:      1         Init-String:
  Number                    Margins            Other
    Print-Number: 1           Left:     4      Space Compression: No
    Start-Page:   1           Right:   76      Attributes:        Yes
    End-Page:   999           Top:      2      Format: As-Displayed
  Breaks:      Yes            Bottom:   2      Top-Labels:
  Wait:         No                             Left-Labels:
  Header:
  Footer:
                                        ──Print Settings: MAIN
```

Fig. 17.1 Print Settings Sheet.

When you hit the SETTINGS command, you are shown a new menu, which corresponds to the different settings in the print settings sheet. You will probably want to change all of the settings at some point, so it's a good idea to know what they mean. The settings are:

PAGE SOURCE DESTINATION INIT-STRING MARGINS OTHER
NAME QUIT

Special Print Commands

Each of these commands requires specific explanation, so we'll take a look at them individually. First, there is the PAGE MENU:

LENGTH SPACING NUMBER BREAKS WAIT HEADER FOOTER

Task — Change the page length
Command — SERVICES, PRINT, SETTINGS, PAGE, LENGTH
Explanation — The page length can be set in lines. The default setting is 66, which corresponds to an 8 1/2 by 11″ page.

Task — Change the spacing
Command — SERVICES, PRINT, SETTINGS, PAGE, SPACING
Explanation — This allows you to print single, double or triple spacing. This command is used primarily for every type of printing *other than* document printing. The space setting you make when you format the document takes precedence over this space setting.

Task — Change the print number
Command — SERVICES, PRINT, SETTINGS, PAGE, NUMBER
Explanation — You can make three settings here:

PRINT NUMBER — The first number to print

START PAGE — The first page to print

END PAGE — The last page to print

Task — Turn headers, footers and page breaks on or off
Command — SERVICES, PRINT, SETTINGS, BREAKS
Explanation — This is a *toggle* for these services.

Task — Pause between pages for insertion
Command — SERVICES, PRINT, SETTINGS, PAGE, WAIT

Task — Create a header
Command — SERVICES, PRINT, SETTINGS, PAGE, HEADER
Explanation — The header first appears in the menu line at top left, and then in the settings sheet. Be sure to hit **[ENTER]** before **[ESC]**, to enter the header.

Task — Create a footer
Command — SERVICES, PRINT, SETTINGS, PAGE, FOOTER
Explanation — The footer appears first in the menu line at top left, and then in the settings sheet after you hit **[ENTER]**. A page number can be added anywhere in the footer by adding a # .

Task — Add a page number
Explanation — See footer or header above.

Task — Describe a source
Command — SERVICES, PRINT, SETTINGS, SOURCE
Explanation — Symphony is asking what you want to print. If you're printing a document, you can ignore this command (unless you've already entered a source, in which case you may need to cancel it). Your entire document will be printed.

If you are printing a sheet, you will want to specify the range (SOURCE leads to another menu, which has RANGE, DATA BASE, CANCEL). You can either point, or type in the appropriate range to be printed out. (See Chapter 5 on ranges if you have trouble here.)

DATA BASE prints out your data base. (See the chapters on data base for further explanations.)

CANCEL removes any previously set range setting.

Sending A Print-Out

Task — Send a print-out to disk instead of to printer
Command — SERVICES, PRINT, SETTINGS, DESTINATION, FILE
Explanation — Although it may seem strange, you can send a print-out directly to your disk, instead of to your printer. Simply give it a file name.

The advantage with this process is that Symphony prints to the disk in a standard ASCII file, which then can sometimes be read by other word processors. (This file will end up with a .PRN suffix.)

Task — Send a print-out to a range
Command — SERVICES, PRINT, SETTINGS, DESTINATION, RANGE
Explanation — This is used to take a range from a sheet and print it to a single column range in the sheet. (Converts sheet to document.)

Task — Cancel a destination command
Command — SERVICES, PRINT, SETTINGS, DESTINATION, CANCEL

Task — Send other commands directly to the printer
Command — SERVICES, PRINT, SETTINGS, INIT-STRING
Explanation — This allows you to code in a printer command sequence. For example, you could code in the command to print in italics (if your printer had that option). For example, the italic command for Epson printers is decimal 052 (check your printer's manual for the codes it uses). You would enter this with a slash (\ ) and then 052. Several commands can be sent at once in this fashion. (See the instructions on printing under word processing in this book for a further explanation.)

Task — Set margins to be printed
Command — SERVICES, PRINT, SETTINGS, MARGINS
Explanation — You can set the left, right, top and bottom margins using this command. The left and right margins that are set using the FORMAT command in a document, will control the document's *appearance*. The commands given here will control the document's *placement on the page*. (See printing a document, in the word processing chapters, for a further explanation.)

You can also reset to the initial margins, or cancel all margins with this command.

Task — Compress spaces into tabs when printing to a file
Command — SERVICES, PRINT, SETTINGS, OTHER, COMPRESSION
Explanation — This compresses empty spaces into tabs, thus saving memory space.

Task — Turn off special off-screen formatting
Command — SERVICES, PRINT, SETTINGS, OTHER, ATTRIBUTES
Explanation — Perhaps you entered underlining, boldface or other special attributes which you will see only when you print out. This command tells Symphony to disregard them. When the command is *off*, no attributes will print. When it is *on*, all attributes will print.

Specific Printing Tasks

Task — Print formulas as formulas
Command — SERVICES, PRINT, SETTINGS, OTHER, FORMAT
Explanation — The default prints formulas as displayed in cells (which is usually in values). If, however, you want the formula itself printed, use this command.

Task — Print top and left labels
Command — SERVICES, PRINT, SETTINGS, OTHER, TOP/LEFT LABELS
Explanation — You may be printing a sheet onto several pages, and want a particular set of labels to repeat on each page. With this command you can spell out the top and/or left labels that are to be repeated. The TOP LABELS command requires that you designate a row range. The LEFT LABELS command requires that you designate a column range. NO-LABELS cancels the command.

Task — Work with several print settings sheets
Command — SERVICES, PRINT, SETTINGS, NAME
Explanation — Symphony allows you to create a library of print settings sheets. You can specify different print settings in each sheet. Thus, you can create a sheet designed to print with one group of settings, and another sheet designed to print with a different group of settings. Then, when you want a particular print-out, you simply call up the appropriate settings sheet and it's ready to go. *Note*: these settings sheets are for the particular *spreadsheet* (or document) you're working on.

Using settings sheets is discussed in detail in previous chapters, notably 9. Briefly, however, the commands are:

USE — Select from the various settings sheets already created, which one you want to use. (Aim with pointer and **[ENTER]**.)

CREATE — Create a duplicate of the previous settings sheet by entering a new name here. You will now need to change the old settings to new ones.

DELETE — Remove an existing settings sheet.

PREVIOUS — Go to the previous sheet.

NEXT — Go to the next sheet.

INITIAL-SETTINGS — Return to the initial print settings.

RESET — Delete *all* the print settings sheets in the current spreadsheet.

≡Configuring Symphony

After spending some time with Symphony, you'll realize that the program comes with default settings for almost every process.

In some cases, however, the default isn't appropriate for your use. You can permanently change many of the defaults by reconfiguring Symphony.

Task — Reconfigure Symphony
Command — SERVICES, CONFIGURATION
Explanation — Using the menu reached through this command, you can make many *permanent* changes in Symphony. We won't go through each change, since they mimic the temporary changes that can be made, as noted in various parts of the book. (If you're unfamiliar with how to make a particular change, just review the process for making a temporary change. The permanent change is handled similarly. If you're still feeling uncertain, some trial and error will usually help.)

```
Directory to become current at start of session                    MENU
File  Printer  Communications  Document  Window  Help  Auto  Other  Update  Quit

 ┌───────────────────────────────────────────────────────────────────────────┐
 │ File:   A:\                    Document              Window                 │
 │ Printer                          Tab interval:   5     Type: SHEET          │
 │   Type:     1                    Justification:  1     Name:                │
 │   Auto-LF:  No                   Spacing:        1       MAIN               │
 │   Wait:     No                   Left margin:    1     Help: Removable      │
 │   Margins                        Right margin:         Auto-Worksheet:      │
 │     Left:   4      Top:     2    Blanks visible: No                         │
 │     Right: 76      Bottom:  2    CRs visible:    Yes   Clock on Screen:     │
 │   Page-Length: 66                Auto-Justify:   Yes     Standard           │
 │   Init-String:                                        File-Translation:     │
 │ Communications name:                                    IBM or COMPAQ       │
 └──────────────────────────────────────────────────────┴ Configuration Settings ┘
```

Fig. 17.2 Configuration Menu and Display.

When you have finished reconfiguration, make it permanent by striking [**UPDATE**]. However, using [**UPDATE**] immediately creates a new configuration file called SYMPHONY.CNF, which erases any previous file with this name. *If you have previously configured Symphony, updating that configuration destroys the old file.* If you want to save the old file, give it a different name before updating.

Once Symphony has been updated, the current .CNF file will be called up, and your newly installed defaults will then apply each time you use the program. (It's helpful to have the .CNF file on the same disk as the Symphony program.)

Attaching Other Applications

Symphony allows other compatible programs to be attached. One example is the Help/Tutorial program which comes with the Symphony package that you purchase.

The attachment procedure is quite simple. In fact, if you have the HELP/ TUTORIAL disk in the appropriate drive when you turn on Symphony, it is attached automatically. If you want to attach this or another program while Symphony is running, follow this procedure:

Task — Attach another program to Symphony
Command — SERVICES, APPLICATION
Explanation — This brings up the ATTACH MENU. In order to attach a program, you must have the file SYMPHONY.DYN on the same disk (same directory) as the Symphony program. When you access the attach commands, Symphony uses this file to help configure the add-on program. Here are the attach commands:

ATTACH — Loads the SYMPHONY.DYN program to RAM memory and asks for the name of the program to be attached. (Symphony will display a directory of add-on programs, those with a .APP suffix.)

INVOKE — Calls up the add-on program, once it has been attached to Symphony.

DETACH — Removes an application which had been previously attached from the RAM memory.

CLEAR — Removes *all* add-on applications which had been attached previously.

Note: more than one add-on application can be attached. Each new program is added to your computer's main memory. The result is a drain of available memory space. This is why you should *not* attach a program unless you specifically intend to use it right away. This is especially true if you are using the minimum 320K RAM memory that Symphony requires.

Security

Symphony provides several security systems. They can be somewhat confusing, however, and unless you're quite familiar with them, you could permanently lock yourself out of your own data! Therefore, they must be *used with caution*.

PASSWORD SECURITY — You can lock Symphony so that only the use of a password can gain access to a spreadsheet.

Task — Lock Symphony
Command — SERVICES, SETTINGS, SECURITY
Explanation — You'll be asked to UNLOCK/LOCK the sheet. The default is UNLOCK. If you select LOCK, you will be asked to type in a password. If you use this, remember the exact form of the word you type in!

Now the sheet will be locked. In order to gain access to it, you'll have to use UNLOCK. When you use this command, you'll be asked for the password, and you must type it in exactly the form you entered it. For example, if you originally set the password as ROBERT, and you now type in Robert, you will be refused entry!

Cell Security — You can lock some, or all, of Symphony's cells so that no changes can be made to them. There are two commands here which interact with each other.

Task — Lock all unprotected cells
Command — SERVICES, SETTINGS, GLOBAL PROTECTION, YES
Explanation — This locks all of Symphony's cells, except for those which have specifically been protected from locking (explained below). Nothing can be added or deleted. GLOBAL PROTECTION can be disengaged by issuing the command and selecting the NO option.

Task — Allow changes to be made in specified cells when global protection is on
Command — MENU, RANGE, PROTECT
Explanation — When you issue this command, you are given two options: ALLOW CHANGES and PREVENT CHANGES. If you select ALLOW CHANGES, you must

specify the range of cells for which changes will be allowed. These will then be referred to as the A range. If you select "PREVENT CHANGES", when global protect is on, no cells can be changed.

Index

Symphony Notes

Symphony Notes

Symphony Notes

Symphony Notes

Symphony Notes

Symphony Notes

Symphony Notes

Symphony Notes